THOUGHTFULLY
Ruthless

VAL WRIGHT

THOUGHTFULLY *Ruthless*

THE KEY TO EXPONENTIAL GROWTH

WILEY

For Andy,
for your love, friendship, laughter, and boldness to move across the
other side of the pond, and utmost unwavering confidence in me.

CONTENTS

FOREWORD

In 30 years of executive and entrepreneurial coaching around the globe, I've observed that people tend to begin their day in one of two ways: It's either yet another glorious opportunity for success, exploration, and personal growth; or, it's a long, slow crawl through enemy territory.

Mind-sets inform behavior, whether consciously or subliminally. My dogs' mind-sets are always positive. If there's an open gate, run through it. Many people's mind-sets default to the negative. Let's do an analysis of the rewards and risks of proceeding through a gate unexpectedly found open. Is it a trap? Could there be danger lurking? What resources should we gather?

Of course, by the time these questions are meticulously answered, someone else has launched Uber, invented the iPhone, and won the Super Bowl. "He who hesitates" these days is no longer "lost," but rather a nonperson. In a turbulent world, we need speed and boldness and a carpe diem attitude. The metaphoric gate doesn't remain open for long.

Can you imagine John Donne (and Ernest Hemingway after him) taking the time and analytic intensity to write, "Identifying the populace for whom and not for whom the cacophony in the campanile sounds" instead of "For whom the bell tolls"? Yet in the age of big data and persistent turbulent times, I see too many people *slowing* their pace rather than increasing it.

Val Wright has opened the gates at firms such as Xbox, Starbucks, and Microsoft and then urged talented people through them. For a quarter century, she has fine-tuned what she calls "thoughtfully ruthless" approaches to better create and exploit opportunity by intelligently leveraging time, energy, and resources. She has coached, worked with, and interviewed leaders globally and found the wisdom in what I call *healthy selfishness*: If you don't put your own oxygen mask on first, you're not as able to help others and will eventually be useless.

The filters we are blessed with in the aging process, as the horizon becomes closer and we begin to regret what we might not complete, can be used at much younger ages if you allow yourself the opportunity. Val doesn't assume the reader is damaged—as so many business books do—but does believe that there are behaviors and skills that aren't always understood, let alone utilized at the most propitious moments. That's why suggestions here such as avoiding *regret roulette* and *letting go of the mediocre* seem so obvious and useful, while also so neglected.

I've known Val for several years, and she is one of the true all-stars I've had the pleasure to coach and support. She practices what she preaches, in that she's forthright, fast, and factual. She suggests nothing that she doesn't practice herself and that I've seen a thousand successful people employ consciously or naturally. Val will drive you toward the *conscious competency* of ensuring that the techniques that follow can immediately and pragmatically improve your life and career.

The question that remains is whether you have the thoughtful ruthlessness to do so. That bell tolls for thee. . . .

Alan Weiss, PhD
Author, *Million Dollar Consulting, Million Dollar Maverick,*
and more than 50 other business books

PREFACE

Not enough people can say I feel in control, I am achieving my priorities, I am energized and inspired, and I have discretionary time to use as I choose. Too many people are exhausted, miserable, and focused on the short term. Leaders who are *thoughtfully ruthless* with their time, energy, and resources will catapult themselves ahead of the competition. Unlimited energy, increased discretionary time to use as you choose, and a backup team who support you is your reward for being thoughtfully ruthless.

When I suggest to my executive clients that they need to be more ruthless, I often see them wince. It has connotations of being brutal, selfish, and heartless. Once I explain my definition of thoughtfully ruthless, I get more nods and acknowledgment that this could accelerate results. For me, being thoughtfully ruthless means managing your energy and resources by being direct, being imperturbable, and focusing on the long term, while recognizing that your time is precious and you can control it, ruthlessly.

I have been part of teams that broke the mold and created ground-breaking, innovative products such as Kinect for Xbox. This book will include that story as well as conversations with innovative founders, such as Gregg Glassman, who built the multimillion-dollar business of CrossFit Inc., which created the billion-dollar industry of affiliates, equipment, nutrition, and apparel. After starting as a personal trainer at Gold's Gym, Glassman catapulted his success by being a thoughtfully ruthless leader. You will also hear other executive insider stories, including how Amazon broke into the fashion industry and turned it on its head. Yet this book goes beyond storytelling and includes a tool kit of exercises, assessments, and proven practical ideas that a leader can implement in his or her business immediately to accelerate growth.

I have been accelerating growth for leaders in Fortune 50 companies for the past 23 years, and I have noticed that leaders who become thoughtfully ruthless make faster progress at changing behavior and letting go of lifetime habits. In this book, I share my insights and conversations with executives from Fortune 50 companies and reveal how we did it, including our mistakes, successes, and advice.

The principles in *Thoughtfully Ruthless* go beyond the boardroom; as a mother of three small children, I exemplify being thoughtfully ruthless. This is not about work–life balance; you need to throw away the scales because they constantly cause you to evaluate and question your choices. This is about creating one life that you lead in a thoughtfully ruthless way, and I will share proven techniques to increase discretionary time, energy, and the ability to be imperturbable.

ACKNOWLEDGMENTS

This book would still be floating around my head as a "perhaps-one-day" aspiration if it weren't for the following people:

Jeannene Ray, Heather Brosius, Lauren Freestone, Michael Friedberg, and the team at Wiley. Your thoughtful feedback and great partnership resulted in a book that will transform how executives rapidly grow their businesses.

Alan Weiss, my strategic advisor, author of over 60 books and godfather of the most dramatic vibrant community of consultants, speakers, and authors in the world. Thank you, Alan, for continuously pushing and challenging me, and creating the ultimate community that I learn from every day.

My remarkable circle of clients, colleagues, and friends who kept asking me to write this book and cheered me across the finish line. Your positively relentless optimism is infectious.

My three daughters, Naomi, Keira, and Olivia, whose boundless energy, continuous curiosity, and love for everything adventurous teach me valuable lessons each and every day.

Finally, my mum and dad, for teaching me that anything is possible with the right confidence and support.

Part I

WHY YOU NEED TO BE THOUGHTFULLY RUTHLESS

Chapter 1

THOUGHTFUL *AND* RUTHLESS

THE TRIGGER POINTS FOR THOUGHTFULLY RUTHLESS

My first realization about thoughtfully ruthless leadership occurred when Microsoft took a $1 billion write-off in 2007 for the *red-ring-of-death* quality problems with Xbox. I was part of the Xbox leadership team, and we were in danger of becoming irrelevant unless we broke away from our strict focus on 16 to 22-year-old men in North America who liked shooting and racing games.

Don Mattrick became the new CEO of Xbox, and he epitomized a thoughtfully ruthless leader. In my first meeting with him, he said, "Val, what are your top ten priorities?" I rattled off five, but then he interrupted me and said, "Here are mine, and here are five more for you that you need to add to your list." Every morning Don thought of the three biggest issues that prevented him growing his business and focused on those that day. He monopolized meetings to drive his agenda, which frustrated everyone around him, but he focused on the goals of the business, ruthlessly and relentlessly. We learned how to make meetings more effective by building *Don time* into the agenda wherein he could share his thoughts and ideas, but the team could still cover the topics that needed to get decided as a group. He knew how to not get sucked into the tactical day-to-day execution and stay focused on long-term strategy.

When I shared some of my views on the leadership team and the changes that needed to happen for us to turn around the business, he said, "Let's spend a day on this next week." I went to his home in Vancouver, Canada, and we talked for a day about how the business would grow in the next three years and what the implications would be for the leadership and organization. We created a plan for what we would change when. That became the basis for the three-year plan for the Xbox business.

Don made his first million dollars at the age of 17 when Electronic Arts bought his games company. He turned around Xbox from a billion-dollar loss to a multibillion-dollar profit. Don is the embodiment of a thoughtfully ruthless leader.

My second trigger happened in South Lake Union, a neighborhood in downtown Seattle that had been transformed when Amazon moved its headquarters and 15,000 employees there. In my first week at Amazon as the human resources director for the fashion business, I spent time with a cross section of people to understand the business and the culture. I asked everyone the same two questions: (1) "What does it take to be successful here?" (2) "What advice do you have for someone new?" one of the buyers gave me the best advice: "Be ruthless with your time, and get used to continually letting people down." That phrase stuck with me as I learned more about the Amazon culture, which moves at lightning speed while orbiting around one central force: the customer.

When I worked at Land Rover in England, our planning meetings were in four-year increments; we reviewed monthly and quarterly sales, faxed from the various global dealerships. There was a huge contrast! Land Rover was compiling data from faxes, whereas with Amazon customer behavior was analyzed by the keystroke, within seconds and often instantly, so you had to move fast. Pixel-level decisions were made to appear on the Amazon home page (the gateway) and each subsequent page, which are then analyzed to determine the success or failure of a product or promotion. Priorities change, and you have to be able to make on-the-spot decisions for where you will focus your own time and how you will lead your team. I learned to become more ruthless.

The final trigger happened the day I brought my twin daughters home from the hospital. My eldest daughter was 23 months old, making me the mother of three daughters under the age of 2. Just like a juggler learns to juggle with more and more balls, I quickly learned to meet the demands of two newborns and a toddler, returning to work as an executive at Microsoft after six months of time off. The secret, I discovered, was being ruthless with my own time, energy, and resources. My husband and I had to ruthlessly make sacrifices. What could we do personally, or where could we outsource? Obviously, we would outsource noncore activities, such as folding and organizing laundry, and use that precious time to play with our daughters. We had to be ruthless.

I first wrote about being thoughtfully ruthless when I launched my own consulting practice. It was the first special report I wrote, and I have had resounding feedback from my clients about its impact. This idea packs a punch, but first let's explore what happens if you are only thoughtful or only ruthless.

WHO IS THOUGHTFUL? WHO IS RUTHLESS?

If I were to ask you to think of a thoughtful leader, it would likely be easy for you. A thoughtful leader knows everyone's name and wants to be liked by everyone. And everyone does like such a leader, until it is decision time, when the thoughtful leader sees a fast-approaching wall and slams the brakes on hard and stalls. Tough decisions often paralyze thoughtful leaders.

One leader I worked with used to deliberate for weeks over decisions that could have been made in minutes! When I asked him what was causing the delay, he said, "Val, this decision won't be popular, so I am trying to figure out a way to make it more palatable for everyone." Even during team meetings, members of the team would say, "It's time to make a decision; let's make the call right now." But still delays occurred, and the competition raced ahead while his team got more frustrated with inaction, and his reputation suffered. Thoughtful leaders are often loved most by junior employees, tolerated by managers, and loathed by executives.

Thoughtfulness is drummed into us from an early age:

- Think about others before yourself.
- Don't hurt someone's feelings.
- Go to your room and think about what you have done.

These are all phrases most of us have heard growing up, so when it is time to be a little less thoughtful, no wonder it can feel so out of character.

There are three definitions of thoughtful leaders:

1. They consider the intended and unintended consequences of their actions.
2. They deliberately focus time and attention on the needs of others.
3. They are reflective of past results so they can repeat successes and learn from failure.

Now think of a ruthless leader. I'm sure you can think of one or two. You may already be scowling. A ruthless leader appears not to care about the implications of their actions and will regularly put their needs in front of others, either consciously or unconsciously. Ruthless leaders are not always liked, but they are often respected.

The serial executive investor Carl Icahn is a ruthless leader. From a distance, he is a disrupter, ruthlessly shaking up the companies he invests in and the boards he is a member of.

There are three definitions of a ruthless leader:

1. They make bold, sweeping decisions.
2. They pay no regard to how people may react to them.
3. They provide unfiltered and often unsolicited feedback at every opportunity.

Ruthless leaders are often loathed by more junior employees, feared by managers, and respected by executives.

CAN YOU NAME ONE?

The far more interesting question is whether you can name a thoughtfully ruthless leader. They are neither too thoughtful nor too ruthless but intentionally spend their time, energy, and resources to reach their goals. They are the ones who have catapulted themselves ahead of their peers and the competition. You may be pleased to hear this is not like a permanent tattoo. It is a state of mind, a learnable (and forgettable) trait, so there is hope. The impact of being too thoughtful or too ruthless will either put the brakes on your company's results, drive your employees crazy, or drive yourself insane.

I have worked alongside some of the top leaders in the world's most innovative companies, and I have seen the brilliant, the mediocre, and the downright cringe-inducing actions of leaders. Those actions have left either a shambolic wake or phenomenal results that redefined how we play and interact with technology.

Thoughtfully ruthless leaders do not leave their business results to chance. Every decision is deliberate and every moment is purposeful. They do not worry whether everyone will like them or agree with them. Making people happy isn't one of their goals; yet, they attract and retain happy people because of their relentless focus and predictable business success. Many leaders focus on the market conditions or the competition as reasons for lack of growth. Yet the single biggest variant is the leader and how they prioritize their time and energy personally, with their leadership team and with the rest of the organization. It's easy to get sucked into the current issues of today's customers, products, and financial results, but leaders who know how to dedicate time to looking ahead one to three years will outpace their competition.

The thoughtfully ruthless leader has confidence, happiness, and clarity on his or her life priorities that nothing and no one is permitted to interfere with. It was unheard of for an executive from Microsoft to work remotely; yet, Don Mattrick made that a condition of accepting the CEO of Xbox role. He would remain based in Vancouver, Canada, and travel to Redmond, Washington, two or three days a week. Don prioritized his family time and taught the leadership team how to work remotely and that being present at the office wasn't a factor in galvanizing a leadership team to transform the Xbox business.

By now, you may be wondering what being thoughtfully ruthless with your time, energy, and resources really means and the impact it will have on your life and business. Let's explore that now.

YOUR TIME, ENERGY, AND RESOURCES

Thoughtfully Ruthless with Your Time

In a constantly connected world, delivering real-time information and keeping up with e-mail, texts, tweets, posts, shares, likes, and pins can seem as futile as sweeping up a pile of leaves on a windy day. You get a fleeting, brief moment of satisfaction, but then the technical wind blows, and you

are back where you started with the important and unimportant demanding your attention, like a new pile of leaves in front of you. A spontaneous
approach to managing your time will not work, not unless it is scheduled
and planned spontaneity is built into your overall plan! If you do not value
your own time and plan it in a thoughtfully ruthless way, then other people
won't either. Many leaders I work with to improve performance tell me that
they don't have enough time at work, and they are frustrated that they don't
have enough time to spend on their favorite activities at home. At this
point, I usually share a little secret, and it is one that some people have to
hear several times to believe. I will share it here, since you paid the cost of
admission:

> **You** are the single greatest barrier to spending your time as you
> want to.

At this point, many leaders go on to tell me how their company, boss,
job, project, and life are different; how I couldn't possibly understand; and
how they would love to change, but it is just not possible right now. I then
refer them to my thoughtfully ruthless secret.

Many people have their e-mail set to populate their laptop or their
phone with new messages every few minutes. You would never get any
work done if you let people knock on your door every 120 seconds, but
that is what you are doing with your e-mail, unless you control when and
how you receive your messages. Many of you will likely have a version of
a to-do list when what you really need is a to-don't list to prevent you from
focusing on the wrong activities. Great intentions are never enough, you
need the discipline to commit and to make it happen. I often work with
leaders to create a *lost discipline list*, which I designed to help leaders
understand why they haven't achieved past goals and what got in the way.
You can sometimes create this in five minutes, though it may take longer
if you truly don't know why you don't achieve what you set out to achieve.
You may also need to discuss it with someone who can give candid
feedback.

If you are not careful, it is easy for your calendar to take on a life of its
own or for your multiple virtual in-boxes to take over your time. But leaders
who are thoughtfully ruthless dedicate specific times of the day to respond
to their complete virtual in-box and to systematically plan their calendar to
accelerate their strategic goals, rather than being victimized by time and

circumstance. Many leaders get dragged into the here and now of everyday execution, therefore neglecting to look at the horizon months or years out. Thoughtfully ruthless leaders dedicate time to considering strategic options and alternative scenarios for their business so they can accelerate growth faster than the competition.

Being thoughtfully ruthless with your time also means being in a job that plays to your strengths, that inspires and energizes you. Otherwise, you are simply wasting a precious opportunity to develop different experiences and skills.

Because we all want more time for what matters most to us, I am always on the lookout for those who successfully achieve that. When I worked with Robbie Bach at Xbox, he was the president of the Entertainment and Devices Division. He was well known for protecting his family time—he was home for dinner every evening and coached his three children's basketball teams. I asked him if he always had this approach and how he maintained it during some highly successful and highly turbulent times at Microsoft.

In my early years at Microsoft I was working incredibly hard and long hours and eventually it became too much. I considered quitting. Back in the early days, there was no remote e-mail access, so working late meant being in the office and that took its toll. A life coach I was working with told me I needed to get control of my life. So he helped me develop a plan where I would always be home for breakfast and dinner, I would coach my kids' basketball teams, and I planned all of my travel domestically and internationally nine months in advance. I created a system: I would travel twice a year to publishers around the world. They knew when to expect me, and if they needed my personal time outside of that, we would talk on the phone, meet at a conference, or they would come and visit me in Redmond. The day-to-day meetings that I ran were easy to control. It was harder if it wasn't my meeting, but I had to get used to just walking out of meetings at 5:30 and telling people that we needed to reconvene.

Clearly, Robbie was both thoughtful and ruthless with his time.

With 153,650 books on time management available on Amazon today, something is missing though. It is not enough to be thoughtfully ruthless with your time. You have to be thoughtfully ruthless with your energy and resources, too.

Thoughtfully Ruthless with Your Energy

I have noticed a recent trend with some executives that I work with. Many are telling me they are exhausted, overwhelmed, and not spending their energy where they would like to. This leads to them being miserable, no longer inspiring their teams, and even unproductive. High-performing leaders often leap from one significant all-consuming project to another without taking a moment to breathe in between. It isn't possible to run a marathon as a connected series of 100-meter sprints; your body couldn't handle the pace and intensity. Yet leaders push themselves and their teams to do the corporate equivalent and then are surprised when people burn out and quit.

Google's CFO Patrick Pichette mentioned in his resignation letter that he wanted to climb mountains with his wife, but not every executive has to quit to lead the life they want to lead right now. They just need to manage their energy in a thoughtfully ruthless way.

There are three critical ways to becoming more ruthless in a thoughtful way with your energy:

1. Be sure you are in your perfect job doing perfect work.

    Your role may have evolved from when you first accepted it, your business may have significantly grown or declined, or you may have new responsibilities. This is why you need to periodically ask yourself what makes your eyes sparkle in your ideal job and whether you are in it right now.

2. Check your ROE.

    Business leaders know about return on investment, but they rarely know about return on energy. Do you spend excessive energy on thoughts, activities, purchases, possibilities, or pondering that is simply not worth the effort? Wasted energy can't be retrieved; it is gone forever. Children are a great role model here; they do before they think and waste very little effort considering or contemplating. If you can be more ruthless by not wasting energy on unimportant thoughts, you will free up your capacity to focus your energy to spend elsewhere. Companies need to do this just as much as individual leaders. One example of this wasted energy with little return occurred at a video games studio where I used to work. The energy wasted on an easy-to-solve problem baffled me. Not only did this waste energy of employees complaining about the lack of music, it also was unproductive, as employees couldn't concentrate or be creative because there was too much distraction and background noise in shared office space.

When Microsoft bought the Rare Games Studio from the three founding brothers, they were making games for Nintendo. Xbox bought them to broaden the types of games you could play on the Xbox. I joined them to manage the transition after the acquisition. Rare Games was a company of musicians, artists, and animators in a small village in the middle of the British countryside. Xbox was part of the (then) largest company in the world. When I talked to employees about what changes they would like to see to help them make better games, almost all said, "We want to be able to listen to music when we work."

Working creatively requires focus, attention, and inspiration, and that was sometimes hard in wide-open barns that housed each game team. What I thought would be a simple and fast resolution had history and complexity behind it. Teams had previously been allowed to listen to music, but on one fateful day, one of the founders was trying to talk to one of the members of the games team and he didn't respond because he had headphones on. That was the day that the music stopped, and nobody thought that it would ever change back due to the determined nature of one of the founding brothers. It took some persuading, but eventually the leadership team agreed to bring back music. During my tenure, I introduced several changes and new benefits, and I increased communication and training, but what I still am known for is bringing back the music.

When I visit a new client, I like to stand in the coffee line and listen in the hallways. What I hear indicates where people are spending their energy. Are they talking about customers, products, and profits or drama, hearsay, and complaining? What would be the equivalent to music while you work in your organization?

3. Burst your bubble.

It is easy to stay inside of your bubble. Inside your bubble are your longtime friends, your trusted work colleagues, and people you know well. It is comfortable and easy, but frankly, it won't continually stretch, grow, and energize you. You see it at every conference and trade show you attend: the same people connect and socialize with the same people. But if you want to stay energized and inspired, you have to burst your bubble of comfort and continually strive to expand your circle of influence at work and in your personal life, in what you read and listen to, and in the events you attend. How many of the business colleagues and close confidants you have today did you met in the last 12 months? If you are always with the same people, you won't get inspired with new ideas, experiences, and growth opportunities.

Knowing who you aspire to be connected to and focusing on getting the right introductions will rapidly catapult your success as a thoughtfully ruthless leader. When I quit my corporate career to launch my own consulting business, I had one great fear: I didn't know anyone in my network who I aspired to be. I needed to seriously upgrade my network of thought leaders who had successful solo practices. I joined the Million Dollar Consulting community and immediately found what I needed and was looking for. The community that Alan Weiss has created is a remarkable place for getting connected with other thought leaders and learning from those who were already successful solo entrepreneurs. Now I have established many great new friendships, peers, and mentors who have helped me rapidly grow my business.

Chapters 7 and 8 further explore how you can be thoughtfully ruthless with your energy.

Thoughtfully Ruthless with Your Resources

Imagine your company two years from now; how much will you grow? What will be your revenue, profit, services, and products? Now, look at your current leadership team and organization. How would you rate yourself on a scale of 1 to 10 in regard to your capacity and capability to lead that future organization? If the answer came very easily to you, then already you have a head start on many of your peers who simply get too caught up in the immediate needs of their business to even start to think about their future business.

CrossFit founder Greg Glassman went from being a personal trainer at Gold's Gym to building a multimillion-dollar business and creating a billion-dollar industry. He told me, "Leading a business in high growth is like operating a rocket ship where you have to change how you operate it on the ground, at 5,000 feet, 10,000 feet, and 100,000 feet. Only a select few leaders can adjust to the altitude change and succeed."

Many start-ups forget about the lofty goals and timeline they set out in their pitch documents and immediately get sucked into execution, which undoubtedly leads to missed deadlines and disappointed investors.

Mismatched employees are one of the top distractions for many of the leaders I work with. Incompatible leaders spend months or years on the wrong leadership team in the wrong job with the wrong priorities. They are miserable, and their teams often are, too; yet, rarely does the situation get resolved as quickly as it could. I have never had a leader say that they regret acting too fast with a decision about their people, but I have met those who regret acting too slowly. Hesitancy often prevents action when leaders are faced with someone on their team who has incompatible skills or the business has simply outgrown them. This misery usually occurs when the leader has not spent enough time on team assessment and action to rebuild the team. You may have a great team that can deliver results, but the differentiation that creates breakthrough results can be determined by one simple question: *Do you have two potential successors on your team who could take your job?*

If you don't have two potential successors, you will fail to scale personally, and your business growth will be held back. You cannot grow and take on new responsibilities if you don't have strong successors to delegate to. Thoughtfully ruthless leaders will make it their number one priority to build and galvanize their leadership team in the first 60 days. You can learn exactly how to do that in Chapter 9; skip there now if you cannot wait.

I was walking around a fast-growing start-up in Silicon Valley in 2015. The CEO was giving me a tour, and he was telling me a third story about how his company used to be a year ago—how it was small enough that everyone could sit around one table for lunch, and now it was really difficult because his team had expanded and was spread out over two floors of his building. I stopped him and asked how he saw his business growing in two years. I flummoxed him. He couldn't answer. I suggested to him that he needed to create powerful stories about the future and tell those stories because that is what will inspire and motivate his team to grow. This isn't much different from what I'm teaching my daughter about how to ride her bike: you have to look where you are going, not where you have been; otherwise, you will crash into an unexpected obstacle.

Being thoughtfully ruthless with your time and energy will create incredible strength, but unless you also focus on your resources, you will fail to scale your business. Focusing on resources will help you to reinvent how you lead as your company grows.

One example of a desperately needed reinvention was when Xbox had just written off $1 billion for quality problems with Xbox 360, and Nintendo's Wii was the hot item for the holidays in 2006. Xbox had a reputation as a hard-core gaming device that was close to becoming irrelevant outside North American teenage boys.

I worked with the Xbox leadership team to create a radical approach to achieving the goal of broadening the appeal of the Xbox from a narrow demographic of gamers that liked to race cars and shoot things to a broad, appealing family-entertainment device. I designed and facilitated an innovation program to broaden the minds and possibilities for Xbox.

We brought together a diverse group of leaders, partners, and creative and technical experts to a remote location and broke every cultural rule in the Microsoft book of doing business: no laptops, no PowerPoint, and no spreadsheets. Invitations were earned by expertise, not seniority in the business. We engaged in three days of play, immersing ourselves in customers' lives, competitors' products, and the broader entertainment industry. Small teams had artists to visually capture thoughts and ideas. A science fair midway through allowed people to hear others' ideas and build on them (not ridicule or trash them). It culminated in a verbal pitch session venture capitalist-style to a panel of executives back on campus at the end of the week. One of the ideas was for a 3D camera that you could control with your body and your voice. This is how Kinect—which sold 10 million devices in three months, setting a new Guinness Book of World Records for the fastest-selling device of all time—was born. Kinect has now sold 20 million devices and repositioned Xbox as an entertainment hub for the living room.

It is not enough to simply know your vision; you have to create understanding and belief within your leadership team, organization, and investors. This generates agreement about use of resources. Friction can occur when there is confusion about the current strategy and the plan to get there. You hold a powerful role in galvanizing your team around the strategy and engaging and inspiring everyone behind it.

HOW THOUGHTFULLY RUTHLESS ARE YOU?

By now, you may have a picture in your head of how thoughtfully ruthless you are. To help you gain a more accurate understanding, I am sharing my assessment here so you can find out for yourself. In my work with CEOs, leaders, and entrepreneurs, I developed a leadership assessment that I use at the start of many of my partnerships. I have provided a shortened version here. For complimentary access to the full version, go to www.valwrightconsulting.com/thoughtfullyruthless. Follow the directions, and see where you fall on the thoughtfully ruthless spectrum.

Rate each question:
 1: Strongly disagree
 2: Disagree
 3: Neither agree/disagree
 4: Agree
 5: Strongly agree

Section A
1. I am satisfied with my discretionary time._____
2. I am proactive with meeting commitments and rarely miss deadlines._____
3. I have regular slots of open space on my calendar._____

Section B
1. I am energized and inspired at work._____
2. I surround myself with people who inspire me, energize me, and make me laugh._____
3. I have an enviable inner circle of advisors who offer me support and candid feedback._____

Section C
1. I am thoughtfully ruthless with the allocation of budget and people to deliver priorities._____
2. I hold the bar high for my team and take appropriate corrective action._____

3. I have a vision and plan for how my organization will grow in the next two years._____

4. I reward achievements that accelerate company, team, and individual goals, in that order._____

Calculating Your Thoughtfully Ruthless^{SM} Leadership Score

First take your score for each section, then calculate your thoughtfully ruthless percentage scores for each section and overall.

	Score	%
A – I am Thoughtfully Ruthless with my time	__/15	
B – I am Thoughtfully Ruthless with my energy	__/15	
C – I am Thoughtfully Ruthless with my resources	__/20	
I am a Thoughtfully Ruthless leader	__/50	

Interpreting Your Results

> 80%—Congratulations, you are a thoughtfully ruthless leader; you know how you focus your time, energy, and resources. The rest of this book will show you how you can further capitalize on these strengths and continue to grow your business. You may have individual questions to focus on. But don't stop reading this book now; you will still learn valuable lessons and benefit from the exercises. You can also get your team to complete this assessment, and you can help them become just as thoughtfully ruthless as you!

41–79%—You have areas in which you are not being thoughtfully ruthless. Identify which are causing you the greatest pain or those that are the quickest to change and implement them tomorrow. Once those changes are in place, pick another two and focus on those and continue until you are satisfied.

< 40%—Watch out, you are out of control! You are at risk of burning out, failing, and driving your organization crazy. Talk through your results with someone you trust and build a fast plan for addressing the top two areas of concern for you. Skip to Chapter 8 for some immediate action steps.

If you want a more in-depth version of this thoughtfully ruthless leadership assessment, go to www.valwrightconsulting.com/thoughtfullyruthless.

What does it mean if you are strong in one section and weak in another? If you have strength in all three areas, congratulations. Often leaders have one or two areas that need greater focus and attention (see Figure 1.1).

Fail to Scale
If you are thoughtfully ruthless with your time and energy but not your resources, it is likely that you will fail to scale personally, and your company will not grow as fast as it potentially could.

Miserable Burnout
If you are thoughtfully ruthless with your time and resources but not your energy, you will likely be miserable and close to burnout. I see this with many high-achieving executives. They can relentlessly dedicate their time to growing and investing in their business, but they put their business too far ahead of their personal needs and hit a wall of performance that they sometimes struggle to recover from without help.

Exhausted Workaholic
If you are thoughtfully ruthless with your energy and resources but not your time, you likely have an efficient, future-focused organization, and you are inspired and energized, but you probably are a workaholic or a martyr. The

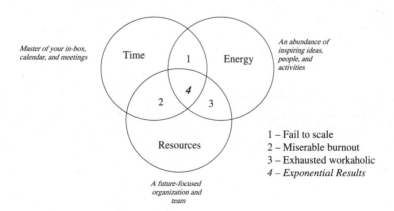

Figure 1.1   The Thoughtfully Ruthless Trifecta

danger is you are setting a terrible example, and it is unlikely that you can sustain this over a long period of time without making yourself ill.

Once my clients have completed this assessment, they then dream of the possibilities for their ideal life. We create their ideal approach to their work and their life, dreaming of the perfect day, week, and year—along with their ideal allocation of time—and compare it to their current reality. I share this along with other practical tools for increasing your thoughtfully ruthless scores in Chapter 11. Go ahead and skip to there now if you cannot wait.

Chapter 2

THE COST OF DOING NOTHING

W e are all taught from a young age to be cautious and studious: Watch your step, don't run with scissors, practice those violin lessons, study every possible topic in case it comes up in your exam. But this obsessive overreliance on being too thoughtful can ingrain behavior and habits that are too cautious. This deep-seated behavior continues to show up in the workplace, resulting in leaders who become frozen with inaction because they want to make sure they make the *right* decision rather than a decision.

This chapter explores the cost of delaying action and the reasons why understanding what's behind your procrastination can be the secret to becoming more thoughtfully ruthless. People strongly fear taking the wrong step, but rarely do I hear complaints from leaders who have made the wrong choices or too hasty choices. The regrets I hear are about inaction and indecision. If you know and understand what causes you to lose your discipline by creating your *lost discipline list*, then you can avoid sliding down the desperate spiral of gloom. This will help you shatter bad habits and embrace new ones, at record speed.

What is the cost of not acting fast enough? Perhaps Microsoft could have beaten Apple in the mobile space or had a greater probability of getting ahead sooner? While hindsight is easy, especially a decade later when you see how the market has played out, Robbie Bach, author of *Xbox Revisited* and former president of Entertainment and Devices at Microsoft, knows all about the consequences of not acting quickly enough.

The technology for touch was there long before any iPad or iPhone. Microsoft was a leader in mobile operating systems along with Blackberry and had experimented with touch for a number of years. Robbie recalls one people review meeting with Steve Ballmer in which there was a full review of the talent on Bach's team: "Steve and I had a conversation if we had the right people on the mobile team. We decided to let them have another six months, to finish the product we had in development, but I knew the feature set was wrong and we didn't have touch capabilities. That was a big mistake." Now in his role as board advisor, this is one of the top pieces of advice he gives the boards and civic institutions he works with: "Fear of disruption, missing a delivery date, ripping a team apart versus giving them another chance and hoping they grow into it is a fatal flaw." Bach now wishes he had demanded access to the best talent in the company to build the mobile business. But he wasn't ruthless enough and couldn't run afoul of his natural tendency to do good by people. "I should have trusted my gut. I knew it wasn't the right team, and that is the advice I now give other CEOs on the boards I sit on."

Robbie demonstrates an incredible trait of being self-reflective and knowing where his blind spots are.

THE COST OF DELAY

Consider a recent decision that you delayed making and ask yourself this: What was the business impact of that decision? Here are some prompts: An increase in sales? A reduction in cost? A missed acquisition? A financial mistake? Some of the common impacts of delayed decision making include a lost customer, a competitor winning over your best customer, a missed opportunity for additional sales, and missed opportunities for add-on services. Delayed decision making usually comes at a high cost. Let's examine a way to calculate that cost, which hopefully will inspire you to increased speed and action.

Calculate Your Cost of Doing Nothing (CODN)

$$\frac{\text{Business Impact \$BI}}{365}$$

BI = business impact
K = date you knew what to do
D = date you actually took action

Add up all of the impacts of your delayed decisions to calculate your BI, and then divide that number by 365. Next, remember the date when you first knew what to do but you waited and the date on which you finally took action. Subtract D from K to get your actual days of delay. Then multiply that number by your daily BI to get your total cost of doing nothing.

Right before I am about to submit a new proposal for working with an executive I ask this question: "What if we weren't talking and you did nothing, what would the cost be?" The answers are always animated and often fascinating. My favorites include: "We would become the next TiVo." "I would be miserable and so would my executive team." "We would lose $500 million in profit." You cannot afford to *not* calculate the cost of your inaction.

Once you have calculated the cost of doing nothing, there is one powerful trait that will determine whether you achieve your goals or not: discipline. Rather than waiting until the end of the year to join the rest of the world reviewing and restating resolutions, you can review your success any time of the year by asking yourself these questions:

1. Take yourself back six months. What hopes and aspirations did you have? What did you achieve? Which did you not achieve? List all the reasons why you didn't. Go beyond easy answers that blame conditions out of your control and focus on what you could have done differently.
2. Use the *toddler why test* by asking yourself why, why, why, but why? Until you get to the cause of what is getting in your way.
3. Ask someone you trust to review your lost discipline list and ask what patterns she sees so you can be sure you are identifying the true root causes of your lost discipline.

The problem is not whether you have goals. You have to know why you are not achieving what you wish you had. If you can't answer that question straight away, then you are wasting your time with your goals, New Year's or otherwise.

THE DOWNWARD SPIRAL OF GLOOM

The downward spiral of gloom can set in when failure to achieve what you set out to, in any part of your life, leads to misery. Once you start on the downward spiral of gloom, it is easy to let healthy eating and exercise habits fall by the wayside, which further adds to your lethargy. If you know your decelerators and accelerators, you will be able to catch yourself before you slip down the spiral and get back on track to achieving what you want. There can be many triggers for hitting the downward spiral of gloom: a new job, a house move, a new boss, a recent acquisition, a new board member.

A common trend in high-growth companies is significant changes in leadership as teams grow and expand. This causes much leadership turmoil that has the potential to trigger a downward spiral of gloom as you figure out your new boss, your peers, and your team members. Chapters 9 and 10 share ideas for ways you can be thoughtfully ruthless with your resources as you build and lead your team through high growth.

Musicians always inspire me, particularly how they assemble teams fast and create inspirational performances. A few years back I was listening to British jazz musician Jamie Cullum at the Blue Notes Jazz Club for the launch of his latest album, *Interlude*. He was incredible. He brought with him five of his regular band members from England, but he also played with an additional 10 musicians who were New York locals, creating a dramatic big band sound in a minuscule venue. If he had not told us, we would never have known that he was playing with strangers by the flow, the passion, and the fun they were all having. Jamie regularly shared the spotlight, and he introduced the whole band to the audience. The crowd was packed in and captivated by the excitement and emotion of the performance. As I watched Jamie perform, I thought about those leaders with new teams, new bosses trying to figure out how to work together and how much time they need to assess, think, and reflect before they get on stage and perform. They are cautious. They hold back and don't always raise the bar for performance as fast as they want to, and they don't trust their gut or instinct enough. They take months to evaluate before action. If a musician can jump off an international flight with jet lag and get on stage a few hours later, creating a captivating performance with a group of strangers, why can't leaders quickly deliver results with a new team? It takes speed, confidence, and a little more ruthlessness as you dial back your overly thoughtful nature.

I hit the bottom of my own downward spiral of gloom when I sat on our kitchen floor crying. I was exhausted and frustrated. By American standards, my six months of maternity leave with my twin girls was positively luxurious, but in that first month back to work, it felt terrible. In between sobs, my husband listened as I reaffirmed that my dream would come true of being my own boss and writing a book by the time I was 40. This wasn't the first time we had pressed reset on our lives. My husband had multiple job offers in the first year after our twins were born, and he chose to take the one in which he was able to walk home, leave his work at the office, and be mentally and physically present at home with three kids under the age of two. Sometimes you have to let opportunities pass you by. While I was on maternity leave with our twins, when they were eight weeks old, one executive offered me a promotion and a bigger job on the condition that I cut my maternity leave short and come back to work early. I learned so much about that leader and that business that it caused me to run away fast from that opportunity as I politely declined!

Chapter 7 explains why getting the right sleep, exercise, and nutrition is essential to boosting your energy. CrossFit is my addiction here, and I have learned many valuable lessons from CrossFit to help me—and you— escape the slippery slopes of the downward spiral of gloom.

You Can't Fail If You Don't Try

Trying and failing is better than not trying at all. I take part in the CrossFit Open every year, where I am delighted to appear in the bottom 41 percent of the 11,507 competitors. It is easy to get distracted if you focus on where you are in the race rather than how close you are to the finish line. I am often the last to finish a workout, especially during the CrossFit Open. Rather than focusing on the fact everyone else has finished and I am still eking out my pull-ups, I think about all of the other athletes who decided not to compete. I would rather participate and place last than avoid competing in the first place. Failure shouldn't scare you, but not trying should. Shift your mind-set to appreciate what you are doing, not what you are not.

Measure and Share Success

The CrossFit Open has a worldwide online league table, which records the results of five different workouts over five weeks; anyone can compete in the CrossFit Games Open stages. Whether it is burpees, squats, or deadlifts, everyone knows the rules, how you are evaluated, what it takes to win, and the rewards. What results and key metrics are important to your life and your business and how can you share them with your team? When you are in the downward spiral of gloom, knowing where you stand and how you can improve relative to your own personal records or your peers can give you the boost you need.

Performance during Exhaustion Matters

"I am exhausted" is a phrase I often hear from executives I work with. Exhaustion is inevitable in CrossFit. How you perform when you are exhausted yet three minutes remain on the clock will set you apart from the crowd. Last year during the games, one of my coaches in the final minute just exploded. He managed three ground-to-overhead movements in the last 10 seconds. He performed harder and faster than in the previous nine minutes. That is the definition of an elite athlete. As a leader, it is easy to become overwhelmed, exhausted, and overworked. The key is how you dig into your mental and physical reserves and continue to perform until you reach your business goal or your CrossFit coach calls, "Time!" It is exhausting in your downward spiral of gloom, so you need to know when you are close to the finish line for projects and goals so you know how to perform even when you are exhausted.

Galvanize Your Team around a Common Goal

Anyone and everyone can compete in the CrossFit Open, and the results are broadcast for the world to see. Each year at every CrossFit box, individuals will come together as one team with passion, determination, and energy. Even though the CrossFit Open isn't a team event, every individual has the same goals: to beat her Open score from last year or to hit a new personal record. My wall balls are awful; I know they will likely appear in the Open so I have been working on them (unlike my overhead squats, which still are pathetic!). Even if you appear in the lowly ranks of the table, you know where you were brilliant and what areas you need to work on. This level of alignment, awareness of strengths, aspiration, and camaraderie is the envy of many leaders trying to inspire and motivate their teams. In the spiral of gloom, sometimes individual goals are not motivating enough; you need to look up to your team's goals and get inspiration for what you want to achieve as a team.

Build a Community Where People Want to Belong

Community support and a strong inner circle is covered in more detail in Chapter 8, but CrossFit is a fantastic example of building a strong community. Last year when I moved from Seattle to Los Angeles, I got a recommendation from my old box, CrossFit Belltown, and I joined the CrossFit 626 family in L.A. Immediately, I felt welcomed and inspired— like I belonged. CrossFit may have an image problem to outsiders, which is baggage that events like the all-inclusive Open can help dispel. How is the reputation and reality of your business? When you bring in new employees to your company, how do they feel? It can be lonely when you are in your downward spiral of gloom; finding a community that supports you can give you the support you need when you need it most.

Team Building with a Payoff

Leaders invest millions in ineffective team-building events where you might learn something new about your peers, but do you truly accelerate your understanding and performance against your goals? Maybe you should hold an Engineering Games or a Design Games and create a competition to inspire, motivate, and accelerate innovation? Or perhaps for those who love challenging themselves, you and your team could consider signing up for the CrossFit Open? This will inspire you to break your own spiral of gloom and that of your team members who may need their own boost of inspiration.

THE THOUGHTFULLY RUTHLESS SUCCESS LOOP

Now that you have heard some options for getting out of your doom spiral, it is critical to know how to accelerate your discipline and become conscious of the triggers that cause you to lose it. Doing so can transform your results and your reputation, if you know what to do with the results next (see Figure 2.1).

The *thoughtfully ruthless success loop* will drive the behavior change you are looking to achieve by following the six steps to thoughtfully ruthless changes:

1. Build awareness: Have absolute clarity about what you want to change and why.

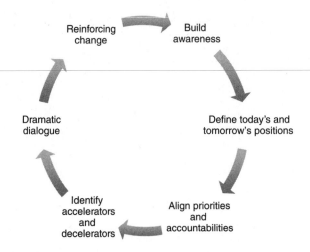

Figure 2.1 The Thoughtfully Ruthless Success Loop

2. Define today's and tomorrow's positions: Know exactly where you are starting from and what your destination is.
3. Align priorities and accountabilities: This is the highest failure point. Those who can influence the change need to be committed and have it as a high priority against every other potential distraction.
4. Identify accelerators and decelerators: Consider your accelerators and decelerators as well as what conditions, triggers, situations, or people speed up or severely hamper your ability to achieve your goals. This may take 10 minutes or a month, depending how honest you are with yourself or whether you have ever given this any thought before.
5. Dramatic dialogue: Unless you are great at talking to yourself in the mirror, often you need to engage someone else to help you see what you can achieve and help you understand what is getting in your way and how to adopt new habits. Use your manager, a mentor, or a coach to provoke, diagnose, and reflect with you.
6. Reinforcing change: Change efforts fail when there is no reward or positive confirmation at the end. The opposite of CODN, cost of doing nothing, is your COS, cost of success. Knowing this and watching it play out positively will help make change stick.

Follow these six steps and then continue with awareness. With any change, especially change in the way you are personally leading, continuous feedback and awareness are the guardrails that will keep you from falling off track.

As you read this book on becoming more thoughtfully ruthless, you may find some aspects helpful and interesting, but a book won't magically transform you by osmosis. The real transformational potential comes right now—in the time you are reading this book and in the 12 hours after you finish it. It is dependent on what action you choose to take. My invitation to you is to pick one thing, anything, and go and do it. Experiment, and then come back and pick one more thing. That process alone will reduce your *worry trifecta* (see Chapter 7) and free up your energy to focus on absorbing new ideas and implementing them fast.

Chapter 3

YOUR SELFISH CHARTER

B etween our teenage years and our senior years, we become desperately
selfless: We try to please our bosses, our partners, our teams, our
coworkers, our children, and our parents—everyone but ourselves. Then,
we wonder why we are mentally and physically exhausted! To find the
balance of perfect freedom and selfishness, we need to adopt the best parts
of the teenage and senior years and become more thoughtfully ruthless.

Do you remember all that sleep you had as a teenager? Endless lie-ins,
time with friends, doing exactly what you liked, whenever you liked,
however you could get away with it? It was *your* music blaring, *your* favorite
food, *your* favorite movies, going where *you* wanted on the weekend.
Teenagers have a reputation for being selfish because they are! They are
self-absorbed, know what they want, and are ruthless with their friendships
and their time. If a teenager doesn't enjoy spending time with someone,
then they don't. Breakups and makeups happen at cheetah-like speed, and
they shake off the drama equally as fast. Teenagers regularly spend time
alone in silence. They also prioritize spending long weekends with friends
they care about.

Let's leap to the other end of the age spectrum: As we get older
something remarkable happens to our tact and diplomacy filter—it
evaporates! The older you get, the less you care about what people think,
and you say precisely what is on your mind. A study by the University of
South Wales proves just that point: inhibition disappears with age. The
study included 41 young adults (aged 18–25) and 39 older adults (aged
65–93) in Sydney, Australia. Each age bracket rated how well their peers

distinguished between personal questions that were okay for public and private talks and how much they self-edited what they should say when. The older adults were freer about bringing up potentially embarrassing topics in public conversations, the study showed. Young adults were less likely to air other people's dirty laundry in public. But they had no problem asking a friend confidential questions in private. "It's not just that older people were more likely than younger people to ask personal questions," says William von Hippel in a news release (School of Psychology, University of Queensland).[1] "In fact, younger people in our study were more likely to ask each other questions of a personal nature, but they usually did so in private," he said. "It seems that young adults have a greater ability to hold their tongue than older adults in contexts where it is inappropriate to discuss personal issues," says von Hippel.

Imagine for a moment this tactful dilemma: Suppose you're having coffee with a close colleague. Your colleague has a personal challenge that may be visible (they just made a glaring error in a board presentation or their suit is really ill-fitting and they would never have made it out of the house like that if they had a mirror with a good view) or unseen (a health condition or family problem). Would you ask that person about that issue in private?

Now, imagine that you and your colleague are sitting across the table from each other at a meeting. Your colleague has the same personal challenge as in the coffee shop scenario. He or she knows the other meeting attendees but doesn't have strong relationships with them. Would you ask your colleague about their private issue in that public setting? Then, imagine the tables were turned. How would you feel if a colleague asked you private questions in the same settings?

The study's design "makes it impossible to know if aging *causes* inappropriateness," write von Hippel and colleagues. Of course, many seniors filter and share information appropriately. But it is a pattern I have observed, and when I shared my theory with colleagues in the medical profession working with senior patients, many wholeheartedly agreed.

I have to agree with Frank Keiser's take on the study. In his blog post on Suddenly Senior, he wrote: "We're simply getting smarter. Why beat

---

[1] J.D. Henry, W. von Hippel, and K. Baynes, "Social Inappropriateness, Executive Control, and Aging," *Psychology and Aging* 24, no. 1 (2009): 239–244. doi:10.1037/a0013423.

around the bush about such things? If you have something to say, say it now and avoid wasting perfectly good brainpower trying to remember to say it later in a more private setting. At our age, who has time for such niceties? Death could find us before we locate that more intimate setting."[2]

You don't have to look hard in many families to find the grandparent who has taken the proverbial truth pill. My proposition is that we could all learn something from this approach to life: Say what you are thinking, stop filtering, and stop worrying about how to say it right or if you will offend or still be liked. Just say it.

So what happens in our thirties, forties, and fifties? We morph into this ever-expanding sponge, absorbing everyone's requests, preferences, demands, and needs. Our own needs and wants go to the back of the line, as long as the never-ending queues at a British post office on pension pickup day.

Forget the midlife crisis. What everyone should be concerned about is the *midlife sponge* effect that will weigh you down, slow you down, and make you downright miserable.

So what can you do to skip from the ruthless approach of your teen years and prematurely fast-forward to the carefree, selfish life of senior years without getting old before your time?

First, you have to create and protect your *power bubble* (see Figure 3.1).

Inside your power bubble are all of the components of what defines your success and happiness: health, fitness, friendships, financial security, silence, image. These will be defined differently for everyone and will be of different sizes and significance. A marathon runner would have a larger fitness bubble than someone who exercises because he knows he needs to but it is not a big part of his life. Outside of the bubble are all of the demand triangles that can pop your bubble and cause you to lose the time and energy dedicated to those priorities. The five critical triangles are family, commitments, OPP (other people's priorities), helping others, and unexpected events.

Although some of the demand triangles cannot be avoided, most are self-inflicted and will cause your power bubble to diminish or pop altogether. Overscheduling is the greatest self-inflicted issue. Just stand at any school gate and listen to parents for five minutes, and you will hear complaints of

---

[2] Frank Kaiser, "Are Seniors Just Rude or Honest?" *Suddenly Senior.* 2005. www .suddenlysenior.com/seniorsrudehonest.html

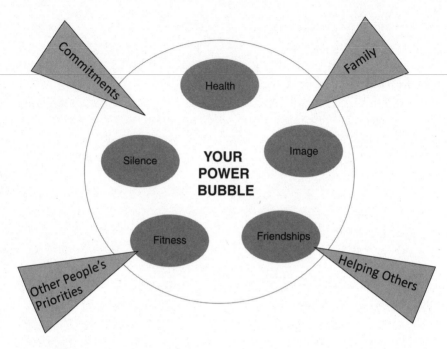

Figure 3.1 Your Power Bubble

the excessive demands of kids' sports practice, piano lessons, and extra-curricular lessons, and that is just the kids' schedule, never mind the parents'. The inability to say no to requests for help, social invitations, and free advice also pops your bubble at the speed of freshly cooking popping corn, but the fundamental issue is that you have yet to sit down and create your own power bubble so you know what is important to you. If you don't know what's important to you, then you can't possibly protect it. To create your own personalized power bubble, you need to create your *sensibly selfish charter*.

YOUR SENSIBLY SELFISH CHARTER

Consider what you want your daily commitments to yourself to be. Daily yoga? Read a book a month? Take the dog on a long walk twice a day? What is your commitment to vacations each year? Then consider what your minimum requirements are for your health, well-being, and mainte-nance (your personal maintenance like chiropractor and spa treatments,

Each day I will:	Each week I will:	Each month I will:	Each year I will:
Friendship rituals:	Couple rituals:	Fitness rituals:	Maintenance rituals:

Development Investments:

Figure 3.2 A Sensibly Selfish Charter

not fixing your drains!). Now look at your friendships: Who do you want to frequently spend time with? Don't forget dedicated rituals for any partners and your me-time. Finally, make a commitment to any personal development experiences that are important to you. Consider that coach you want to invest in, the networking group you want to commit to, or the language you want to learn for your next European holiday. What new skills do you want to learn? By being continually curious, you can learn new skills or take up a new sport—don't settle for the same old routine. Elite athletes are constantly searching for new ways to stretch and grow themselves. Build in goals that stretch your thinking (see Figure 3.2).

Sensibly Selfish Charter

Answer these questions to create your own sensibly selfish charter:

Each day I will:
Each week I will:
Each month I will:
Each year I will:
Maintenance Rituals:
Pampering Rituals:
Friendship Rituals:
Couple Rituals:
Fitness Rituals:
Me-Time Rituals:
Development Investments:

Once you have created your sensibly selfish charter, consider who you need to tell (not ask) about your sensibly selfish charter. Explain why it is important to you and whether you need any support from them to make it happen.

Early in my career, I worked with an executive who was the best in the industry. She was wicked smart and captured the attention of the CEO, our executive team, and our board; yet, every time I met her I was distracted. The truth is she had terrible shoes and hair. Every pair of her heels were permanently scuffed—like should-have-thrown-these-away-but-they-once-were-great-so-I-am-keeping-them terrible. She earned a very hefty salary so she could easily afford a well-kept pair of shoes or three. And her hair looked like she had moved to the area and she hadn't yet found a local hairdresser, but this went on for years. I clearly hadn't learned to channel my inner grandparent and valued my career too much to actually tell her, but everyone talked about it.

That is why image is one of the six foundational bubbles in your power bubble. Your image has to match your actual success or your desired future success. Having worked at technical companies in the United States, I have seen the good, the terrible, and the downright embarrassing style and fashion faux pas—socks and sandals on men, and, worse, flip-flops and shorts with feet up on conference tables. And this was the executives, not just the developers.

I sought out celebrity hair colorist and salon owner Marco Pelusi from Hollywood to get his perspective on how image contributes to someone's mind-set and the impact of their success: "The first thing—literally, the very first thing—that someone sees when they look at you is your *hair*. Not your skin, not your makeup, not your clothing, but your hair. It's the framework for everything about you. If you let your hair go downhill, you will not feel confident, and you will not be at your personal best. That's it—achieving personal best—and that means prioritizing time to look after yourself and make you look the best you can possibly be."

Pelusi works with many of Hollywood's most successful actors, executives, business owners, and entrepreneurs, and he sees a direct correlation between how people take care of their appearance and hair and how that positively affects their mental state, energy, and ultimately their success. "Actors who take the time and spend the money to groom themselves book more work. This has happened time and time again in my world. I have a character actress whose beautiful red curly hair was long and untamed but the moment we gave her a sassy, short cut, she has booked work ever since. I also work with a woman who had been brunette for a very long time. We made her into a blonde, and the response from the casting directors was overwhelming! She's been guest starring on several TV dramas ever since. It is too easy to go into a downward spiral of gloom and not invest in yourself when things aren't going well. Many of us can have dip or a lull in our finances or career. But it's important to keep fresh during those times with our personal appearance, too. The ones who maintain their level of success are selfish enough to not miss a beat with their hair—as they may need to go on an important interview and/or meet up with a very important potential new client or business opportunity. My most successful clients think ahead and plan for their hair color and grooming appointments. The really good ones will specifically plan a hair appointment to be just prior to a major professional event. Timing and planning ahead is everything."

Don't fall into the trap many executives and entrepreneurs fall into: Instead, put your own needs ahead of those of your customers, investors, employees, and everyone else, because if you are an exhausted mess or, worse, sick or in hospital, you will be no use to anyone.

WISHFUL THINKING WORKS

To really become sensibly selfish, you have you know how to wish, not on a star, but on your future, because once you wish, you know what you are aiming for.

I wish I could go to Japan on holiday. I wish I could learn a new language. I wish I could get promoted faster. I wish I could run a marathon. I wish I could launch a new start-up.

There are two types of wishes: empty and intentional. Empty wishes are as close to lies as you can get. Those uttering empty wishes don't actually want them to come true—not enough to make them happen—so they talk about them, moan about them, describe them in an enviable way but all without any intention of making it happen. Empty wishes need to be ignored, but intentional wishes need to be explored, developed, and implemented.

Take a moment to consider the life you want to lead. Many people sit at their corporate desks dreaming about quitting and creating a company, but fewer than 10 percent of those people actually do it. Gavin Price is in that minority. Back in 1999, 19-year-old Gavin joined the Rare Games Studio

as a video games tester. He wasn't wishing back then that 16 years later he
would launch Playtonic, the most successful video games Kickstarter in the
United Kingdom, with $2.9 million of funding. Gavin met Chris Suther-
land on the Banjo-Kazooie team that made the platform game featuring a
bear with a bird in his backpack; it sold over 2 million copies worldwide.
They went on to work together on other games, including Viva Piñata and
the Kinect Sports series, after Microsoft acquired the studio where they
worked for $375 million.

Once things got to the point at which more than 200 people were
needed to make the game, Gavin knew he wanted to step back in time, so
he started his intentional wishful thinking. He wanted to make games again
for gamers, not for the marketing and business leaders. "I wanted to go back
to basics and create a team with no management infrastructure, design
documents, or overhead." Chris Sutherland had learned from his colleagues who quit their corporate jobs before him that many leave their
corporate job and do something completely alien to what they are good at.
Chris reflected, "While this may work for some, I know one of the critical
reasons we have been so successful is because we are sticking to what we
know: making platform games."

Intentional wishful thinking requires you to really understand the
criteria that will make you successful. Gavin and Chris are building a
company based on three fundamental tenets:

1. Quality matters.
    GoldenEye 007 was released one year after the James Bond movie
    came out and became the third best-selling game on Nintendo's N64
    platform at the time, with more than eight million units sold. It is
    hard to imagine a full-year delay on a movie tie-in game today, and
    that is because the marketing voice in decisions is a really loud one.
    GoldenEye was delayed out of the desire to get closer to perfection
    for the gamers playing the game rather than hitting a launch date
    regardless of quality. Gavin intends to use the additional Kickstarter
    funds to de-risk his current planned launch date of their first game, so
    that quality does not have to suffer.
2. Know when to talk to customers and when to shut it off.
    Rare used to make games in complete secret with no public
    relations, press, or external marketing before a game launched. The
    Playtonic team has requested and received thousands of fans' ideas

and feedback—from the size of the Laylee's nose to how the game will play. "We have been delighted with all of the input, but we will then go dark and go and write the game without continual input as we want to create the element of surprise," said Chris.

3. Only plan three steps ahead.

I have seen many business ideas fail in execution because CEOs waste ridiculous amounts of time planning rather than doing. Gavin didn't fall for that trap. "I only plan two or three steps ahead and focus on that. My first priority was getting Chris on board and then other key members of the team. The Kickstarter idea came later in the game." This allowed them to make decisions in real time, so when proposals for different partnerships or ideas came up, Gavin could dedicate time to consider them openly rather than with a fixed view because he had planned so far ahead.

Chris and Gavin were able to make their intentional wishful thinking work because they knew when to be thoughtful and when to be ruthless.

My favorite childhood memory is of long summers with my brother, sister, and mum spent on the beach in a quaint seaside resort, Weston-super-Mare, in England. My mum had a job that allowed her to take summers off, and she spent them with my sister, my brother, and me on the beach. That memory is what I wanted to create for my three daughters who are now seven and five (the five-year-olds are twins). I wanted to create a life that would allow me to take summers off. I knew I wasn't going to get that in corporate life, and so I knew I needed to, at some point, make that leap.

I was in Anchovies and Olives, a new restaurant in Seattle, with two of my friends, and I said to them, "By the time I am 40, I am going to have my own business and have written my own book," I said. "That's the first time I've ever said that aloud. I'm now really scared. Please get me a glass of wine!" I created this plan. It was my crawl-walk-run plan.

I knew that I couldn't leave Microsoft and then launch my own business because I was so indoctrinated into one company culture. I wanted to get a different corporate experience before leaving. So I joined Amazon's Fashion Leadership Team and made my intentional wishful thinking work for me. I spent a year at Amazon, and then I decided to make a leap and launch my own business. I had to—I had told my friends, who were holding me accountable! Then here comes the second part of my intentional wishful thinking: my first book and the proposal for book number two is already written and ready for publishers to consider.

On my journey to creating my own intentional wishful thinking, the most common reaction I received and still receive from others starts with two words—"I wish . . .":

> . . . I wish could do what you have done.
> . . . I wish I had your energy.
> . . . I wish I could quit my job.

I often wonder and sometimes ask whether it is an empty wish or whether they want to create a plan to make their intentional wishful thinking come true. Once you start looking for this in other people, it becomes like a buzzing fridge in the corner of the room that now you hear louder and louder. I suggest that it's not enough to wish. You've got to intentionally wish, then you've got to plan, and then you've got to do.

I'd encourage you all to think about what it is you wish for. What is your intentional wishful thinking? What is the life that you want to create? I do this a lot with business leaders. I ask them to describe their five-year vision: What do you want life to look like in five years' time? I ask them to describe their business in five years' time: How big will it be? What are your customers? What are your leaders? What will the size and scale of your business be in five years? How are you feeling about your current leadership team and the capability and capacity to get there? At that point, one of two extremes happen: I either get gushing and exciting dialogue, and we start discussing the possibilities about how their business can grow faster, or I get a blank look, and they say, "I really don't have time to think about that right now." That's when I say, "Well, really, you should be more thoughtfully ruthless. Let's talk about how you're spending your time and your energy, because if you're not freeing up time to think about where you want to be in five years' time and how you are going to get there, then all of this activity and time you're spending on your day-to-day calendar is focused on the wrong thing." Chapter 9 further explores how you can create what I call your leapfrog organization to make your intentional wishful thinking a reality.

Chapter 4

BECOME BRILLIANT AT DEMONSTRATING YOUR BRILLIANCE

Thoughtfully ruthless leaders know that results alone will not build and sustain incredible success. Your brilliance alone will not endlessly carry you forward in your career. Eventually, it will crash on the shoreline, and you will lose that propulsion if you don't create an endless source of continuous thrust by being brilliant at demonstrating your brilliance. The requirement to demonstrate your brilliance increases exponentially as you accelerate your career. Employees and frontline managers are rewarded and recognized predominantly for their immediate results, whereas CEOs and executives have to pay more attention to how they are demonstrating their results, impact, and value.

You may know you are brilliant, but not know how to effectively demonstrate it, or you may not even be sure how brilliant you are. Try mapping yourself against this assessment. Rate how strong your results are and how well you showcase and demonstrate those results (see Figure 4.1).

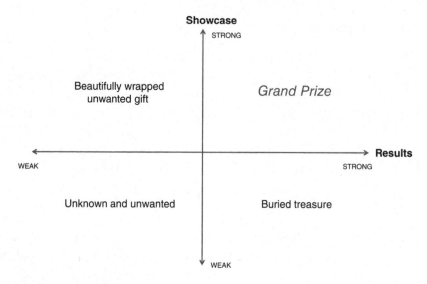

Figure 4.1 Brilliant at Demonstrating Brilliance

ASSESSING YOUR BRILLIANCE AND HOW BRILLIANTLY YOU DEMONSTRATE IT

Unknown and Unwanted

If your results are weak and your demonstration of those results is also weak, you will be unknown and unwanted. You are likely undervalued in your current role, not receiving headhunter calls, and not getting big bonuses or promotions. While it may be hard to recognize yourself in this box, this is often where mismatched employees find themselves. If you are in a job you don't enjoy, isn't making the most of your strengths, and doesn't excite and energize you, then you could find yourself here. The good news is that this is a temporary spot—if you choose to take action fast. Start with identifying what results are expected of you in your role and how you can deliver them; this may be the point at which you decide you are not the right person to deliver those results. Make sure you agree with those on your team about the expected results and how you will measure success. Then set a realistic timeline for improvement and discuss alternative roles or careers if those goals are missed.

Buried Treasure

I have a successful consultant who I mentor. She recently achieved 25 percent of last year's revenue in three weeks. She is increasing her business by over six figures each year; yet, she was completely oblivious to her success. A large focus of our work together is helping her better articulate and showcase her success. She previously operated in a bubble, never stopping to pause, to celebrate success, and to articulate where she is brilliant. If you are like buried treasure, then it's vital that you learn to articulate your thoughtfully ruthless leadership voice (see later in this chapter) and practice sharing it and talking about it. Ask a mentor or your coach to help build a specific plan to increase your shamelessness.

The Beautifully Wrapped Unwanted Gift

I'll never forget unwrapping a beautiful gift bag with intricate ribbons that contained the perfect box with the velvet-lined lid. I remember it so clearly because when I looked inside the box, I found the most garish, brightly colored scarf I had ever seen. It looked as if someone had dropped the paint palette onto the silk screen printer. I smiled politely and said thank you, but secretly I wondered how many times I needed to wear it in front of my boss to express my appreciation for the thoughtful gift, or whether I could hide it in the bottom of my wardrobe and hope they forgot about it. Gift wrap is not always an indication of quality inside. Just like the new CEO whose outer shine may be more dazzling than the results he or she can deliver, surprises happen. Could this be you? Leaders who are unable to follow up on their talk with action often move jobs frequently. Once can be discounted, twice you may need to pay attention, three times is a pattern. Although this may be hard for you to acknowledge and admit for yourself without others giving you feedback, it may be easier for you to identify it within others you work with. If you have people on your team who fall into this category, commend them on how they showcase their work, but challenge them to get specific with how they are delivering results.

This is why turnover among leaders peaks in the first 12 months; that is long enough for the shine to wear off and for promises to start to be measured and decisions made regarding the long-term probability of a successful partnership.

You could also be shining a spotlight on the wrong part of your experience and skills. Complete the thoughtfully ruthless leadership voice to make sure that you know the right points you need to be highlighting so you can divert the energy and attention in the right direction.

Grand Prize

If you are strong at delivering results and strong in showcasing those results, you will be considered the grand prize by your boss, your board, and your shareholders.

WHY APPEARANCE TRUMPS REALITY EVERY TIME

"There is absolutely no way he should be a CEO, Val. He has jumped companies, never delivered, and can't possibly be a CEO," said an executive I was working with. He was telling me about someone he had known for many years—a person who had been a peer and then went on to be a CEO. I told him that the sole reason he was frustrated was because he was seeing someone who was brilliant at demonstrating his brilliance. In fact, the point was that this person could even be masking his inferior brilliance because he was so good at talking about what he thought he was good at.

How many times have you been shocked when someone you know was promoted, hired into a dream job, or received public recognition for their perceived success? In these cases, you are likely witnessing people who are brilliant at demonstrating their brilliance.

Why Being Told I Was Average Was the Greatest Gift I Ever Received

I will never forget my first performance review in the United States. I had been in the states for a year, Microsoft had relocated me from England to Seattle, and I sat in my boss's office for my review. I knew it was going to be good: I had experienced an amazing year and everyone had been telling me I was "awesome!" (a new word for my vocabulary coming from England). I was excited as I sat in my boss's office, but then I was told I was "average." It didn't matter what the numbers were, the message was I was average. I was confused. My manager even promoted me during this performance review, but it didn't matter because I got a score that told me I was average. At Microsoft at that time, everything was competitive. It mattered what score you received each year because you received a *lifetime annual review score* that tracked your scores over the whole of your career, so my average year would follow me for years to come! After the initial shock, I discovered why I was rated as average—because I was not shameless enough. As a humble, British leader in corporate America, I was not shameless enough in talking about my achievements, telling others about my achievements, and loudly proclaiming how brilliant I was.

I was brought up not to shout about my achievements, that you had to work hard and people would just see from your results that you were good. In England, it was considered crass, inappropriate, and braggadocios to talk about how brilliant you were, so I had no clue how to do this. I have found that it is not just some Europeans who struggle to be brilliant about demonstrating their brilliance; many leaders I work with find it difficult, too.

That performance review was just the jolt I needed. I had failed to learn the most fundamental difference between the British and American culture: how you describe and talk about your achievements. I missed that I needed to amp up my positive description of my skills and achievements a hundredfold. Nobody had pointed this out to me, but I had failed to ask and adapt. I needed to learn that *awesome* is not the highest accolade you can receive and that if I didn't start talking about my success and shamelessly sharing my achievements (well beyond my comfort zone) with my boss, other leaders, and my peers, more than I was ever comfortable doing, if I didn't talk about my minor results as though they were major achievements, if I didn't invest time and energy in sharing my results with my boss, my boss's peers, and my peers, then my American colleagues were going to rapidly pass me by.

The Brilliance Barometer

As I recovered from my average year and successfully continued to grow my career, I saw patterns emerge for those leaders who were more successful, got promoted faster, and were tapped to go onto executive and CEO roles in other companies. I developed these insights into the *brilliance barometer* for you to determine how you compare and how you can improve. Use this to assess yourself, and then we'll discuss ways to make improvements in each area (see Figure 4.2).

Leaders who are brilliant at demonstrating their brilliance consistently:

1. Find it easy to talk about results
2. Share stories that demonstrate quantifiable impact
3. Concisely communicate

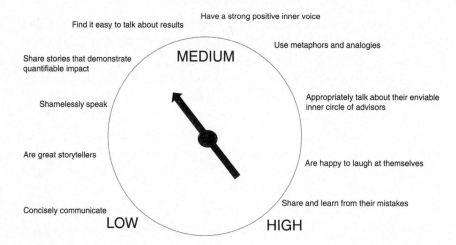

Figure 4.2   The Brilliance Barometer

  4. Have a strong positive inner voice
  5. Are great storytellers
  6. Shamelessly speak
  7. Use metaphors and analogies
  8. Appropriately talk about their enviable inner circle of advisors
  9. Are happy to laugh at themselves
  10. Share and learn from their mistakes

Read though the descriptions of these 10 factors and rate yourself using the following scale:

- Superpower—It comes naturally.
- Energy Sapper—I can do it, but it takes effort and deliberate attention.
- Danger Zone—Others do this much better than I do.

Take credit for your *superpowers*, develop a plan to practice your *energy sappers*, and talk to your mentor or coach about your *danger zone* areas to understand how to overcome them.

  1. Find it easy to talk about your results
     If you were being interviewed on a TV news channel for your industry, could you immediately talk about the results you and

your team have achieved? Do you already have five possibilities running through your mind and are you trying to decide which you would pick, or are you struggling to think of even one example? If your results aren't at the forefront of your thinking, you will not be able to successfully and swiftly tell powerful stories.

2. Share stories that demonstrate quantifiable impact

Do you talk in abstracts and generalities or specifics with financial numbers? What about when you start a new job? Can you quickly quantify your results? I often work with CEOs and executives before they start a new role to help accelerate their impact when they walk in on day one. I was talking with Meredith Amdur, CEO of Wanted Technologies, about her first few months as CEO:

I was unexpectedly confident walking in there on day one. I couldn't have done that without you. The pre-work allowed me to focus completely and gain the self-assurance needed to conquer any dayone fears of communicating a difficult and unexpected leadership change to the team with the right tone and needed assurances. I didn't lose a single person from the key leadership team in the first year, which was just the stability we needed. Our stock price rose nearly 25 percent in the first two months after I took the reins. We hadn't reported earnings, so that market momentum was a vote of early investor confidence in me and the strategy we laid out for the company.

Meredith needed to rapidly demonstrate her brilliance as a new CEO. She not only achieved results but also was able to quantify them in ways that influenced the company.

3. Concisely communicate

Don't use a sentence when a word will do.

Don't use a paragraph when a sentence will do.

Don't use e-mail when picking up the phone will do.

Don't let meetings take 60 minutes when ending early will do.

Don't call a meeting when speaking quickly to two people will do.

4. Have a strong positive inner voice

Take a moment to listen to the voice inside your head. Does it typically sound like your greatest supporter or your worst critic?

You are in full charge of the volume control and the mute button. Make sure you are using it to full effect.

5. Are great storytellers

Vice president of sales for the *Los Angeles Times*, Kate Hill, was pacing up and down trying to get ready for her talk to 300 people the next day. It was 8 PM when I got a message saying, "I need to talk to you. I am dreading an important presentation tomorrow."

Kate was approaching the presentation the way many leaders do: a detailed set of slides on PowerPoint, lots of data, intricate financial numbers, and loads of inspirational sales messages. I asked Kate these questions:

- What is the one message you want people to remember?
- Where were you and how did you feel when you first had this idea?
- What will the cynical people in the room be thinking when you share your talk?

This was Kate's reply:

- What is the one message you want people to remember?
  - We will increase sales and delight our customers introducing a new customer relationship management system
- Where were you and how did you feel when you first had this idea?
  - This is where Kate got excited and animated. I was at my desk late at night going cross-eyed looking at a pile of disjointed spreadsheets trying to track and monitor the sales from our best customers and thought there has to be a better way for our sales team.
- What will the cynical people in the room be thinking when you share your talk?
  - This was Kate's favorite question. She easily rattled off 10 areas in which there would be concerns and cynicism. We prepared by talking about which concerns were unfounded, one that would be unlikely to happen, how many were real concerns that were easy to address, and which were real concerns for which she had no solution.

I suggested to Kate that she ditch her 30-page PowerPoint deck, start with the story of sitting at her desk, and talk just as directly and honestly as she had to me about the founded and unfounded concerns for the changes.

I got a call the following day from Kate saying she went from phobic about speaking to mildly enjoying it. Her boss told her she nailed it, and she now has a new approach to getting her message across when speaking. The way to become a powerful storyteller is to be clear about what you want to leave people with, paint a picture of your views, and confront healthy and unhealthy cynicism.

6. Shamelessly speak

In the last year, where have you told your story, your team's story, or your company's story? Brilliant leaders demonstrate their brilliance by regularly talking to people outside their bubble. In large corporations, this means other groups, locations, divisions, and subsidiaries. At start-ups, this could happen at local entrepreneur groups, venture capital events, and with your local chamber of commerce or industry groups. Share your story, your successes, lessons learned, and make a request for how your audience can help you.

7. Use metaphors and analogies

Listen to Kevin Spacey as Francis Underwood in the Netflix series *House of Cards*. His metaphors are incredible. My favorite was this one: "There is no better way than to overpower a trickle of doubt than with a flood of the naked truth."

8. Appropriately talk about their enviable inner circle of advisors

When Don Mattrick was leader of Xbox, he did this to perfection, often referring to industry moguls, including Steven Spielberg. His list of contact is the strongest I have seen. When making strategic investment decisions, he had immediate access to the best minds to advise him on how Xbox should respond to strategic choices such as expanding into entertainment, the shift to mobile, and broadening the appeal of the Xbox.

9. Are happy to laugh at themselves

Some leaders might cringe with embarrassment if they appeared on the satirical cartoon *South Park*. Not Peter Moore, COO of Electronic Arts; he has a statue of the character proudly displayed in his Bay Area office.

10. Share and learn from their mistakes

Being brilliant at demonstrating your brilliance isn't about bravado and braggadocio. Jeff Bezos demonstrates his brilliance remarkably well, but he is the first to say he made a mistake, not just privately, but publicly outside of the board room, too.

HOW TO TRANSFORM FROM BEING HUMBLE TO SHAMELESS

Now that you know why you need to be brilliant at demonstrating your brilliance, here is how you do it. Many leaders I work with know they need to be more shameless but don't know how to do so—they have never done it before. Follow this guide to capture your thoughtfully ruthless leadership voice, which is the foundation to you becoming more shameless.

Warning!

There are several typical reactions leaders have when completing this exercise: frustration, enlightenment, annoyance, procrastination, and deep thought and reflection are among some of them. There are no right answers, and speed of completion does not define success. You may take 10 minutes or 10 days to complete this, depending on several factors. It is important that you complete it honestly (see Figure 4.3). The explanation

Figure 4.3   Capture Your Thoughtfully Ruthless Leadership Voice 1-3-5-10

of the process follows, and then I share some other tips to help complete and apply it.

1-3-5-10 Your Thoughtfully Ruthless Leadership Voice

1–Sentence That Describes Your Unique Value

In one sentence, describe the unique value that you bring to your company.

Prompts: If this is difficult, try this exercise: Find a quiet place for five minutes, set an alarm if you need to, and spend five minutes writing down 20 sentences that each describe your unique value. Don't stop, keep writing. Once you have finished, reread the sentences, and pick the three that resonate with you the most. Look at the top three and pick one and move on.

3–Distinct Traits

What are the top three distinct traits that set you apart from your peers and competition?

Prompts: If it is hard to define for yourself, ask your board or your boss what makes you unique and why they hired you; then pick the three that resonate with you the most.

5–Proudest Achievements

What are your five proudest achievements in your whole life? The achievements don't have to come from your work life. Did you run a marathon? Did you achieve something radical early in your career?

Prompts: If this doesn't come easy to you, take a walk down your career memory lane, remembering what you achieved in each of your roles and any significant achievements in your whole life.

10–Sound Bites

List the top 10 sound bites that you are known for.

Prompts: This is often the part that many leaders get stuck on. You may need to ask your team, your peers, or previous teams or companies where you have worked. One of mine is "brilliant at demonstrating your brilliance"; another is "look where you are going, not where you have been." Once I realized what a roast was (because in England that is what you eat with your family for Sunday lunch), I discovered a great way to find these sound bites. As you are leaving one team and joining another, ask what phrases you are known for. One leader I used to work for had all of his sound bites printed on a T-shirt as a farewell gift.

Your Reaction

Pay attention to how you feel now that you have completed your thoughtfully ruthless leadership voice. Ask yourself why you feel that way. I always ask this question when I complete this exercise with my clients, and I receive a wide range of reactions. Here are some:

- This helped me realize that I am halfway through reinventing myself. I first answered it how I am today, but then I redid it according to my aspiration and that was more exciting and exhilarating.
- Frustrated. It was painful, and even though I know I should know this, I haven't previously put a lot of thought into this.
- I highlighted personal achievements as my proudest, and then I realized I don't talk about those enough at work and I want to more.
- It made me realize who I am authentically isn't how I portray myself to others, and that gap and disconnect is exhausting me.
- I don't think I have any sound bites. I might, but I don't know what they are.
- I am not using any of my distinct traits in my current company, and I just realized that is why I am not feeling fulfilled right now.

YOUR ACTION

All of the previous reactions are normal and expected. This may take you more time than you think, it could take 10 minutes, 10 days, or longer. The first step of defining your value is often the most insightful. If answering number one is difficult, then it is hard to continue with the rest, but that in and of itself could be a valuable insight for you. One CEO told me as she wrote her unique value statement that it was not what she wanted to be known for and wanted to reinvent herself, so she set about creating a new value statement that described what she wanted to be known for, and it gave her a complete energy boost and hope for the new focus of her work.

Once you have completed your thoughtfully ruthless voice pyramid ask yourself whether it is intentional enough, is it shameless enough, and is it dramatically describing you. Then follow these three steps:

1. Take this and share with your enviable inner circle.
2. Get feedback from your mentor, and peer group.
3. Build feedback in from your clients, customers, and employees.

You can also use the thoughtfully ruthless leadership voice pyramid when you speak at conferences and internal company events, when you articulate your success to your board or leader, when you are interviewed in the media, and in your company blogs, articles, or interviews.

Once you have determined how brilliant you are at demonstrating your brilliance you can also help your team assess themselves and help them increase their impact.

Now you know your thoughtfully ruthless leadership voice and what action you can take to increase how brilliant you are at demonstrating your brilliance, and you can now learn the remarkable two-letter word that will rapidly free up your time and energy.

Part II

THOUGHTFULLY RUTHLESS WITH YOUR TIME

Chapter 5

THE POWER OF NO

There is a weapon of choice that is radically more effective than any other device for creating time and energy; it is one simple word, *no*. This word is not used enough, and when people try to use it, they often translate into fluffy, subjective, and confusing words and phrases, such as *perhaps*, *not right now*, and *let me think about it*. The word *no* is much more effective, and it should be used on a daily basis. This is the area where I see 75 percent of leaders being far too thoughtful when they need to be more ruthless and say no.

I used to work with a vice president who would regularly just walk into product reviews and share his opinion with teams farther down in his organization. He did it because he loved to see the products in development at an early stage, but his comments were distracting and confusing to junior members of the team and would undermine the managers leading the functions. Once the vice president realized that his interference was not only unwelcome but also unproductive, he told his team that they had permission to tell him no when he asked to attend meetings or when he started diving down too deeply into the organization.

Many time management approaches tell you to focus on prioritization, organization, and delegation when the fastest way you can free up additional time is learn to say no more often to the intentionally right topics and people.

Take a look at the following five categories of focus and determine where you find it easy and hard to say no.

Rate yourself using the following scale:

1. I dive too deep and get too involved.
2. I am involved at the right level, occasionally saying yes too much.
3. I ruthlessly know when to say no.

Area	Rating	Comments
1. Product and services discussions		
2. Customers		
3. Investors/your board		
4. Employees		
5. Social commitments		

Now that you have rated yourself in each of the areas, pick one to work on first and experiment with saying no more often.

THE POWERFUL POST-IT

There is a secret I use with all of my clients that I haven't shared with anyone else. It is a technique that surprises them and usually causes them to laugh at the ridiculousness of it; many tell me initially that it just won't work. I ask them to entertain me and prove me wrong, and every time I hear that it was exactly what they needed, which is no surprise to me.

When executives are asking for advice about how to learn to stop a particular behavior, or to learn to say no more, they tell me all the things they are thinking. I ask them to grab a Post-it and write these three words on it:

JUST
STOP
IT

I ask them to put the Post-it at eye level on their computer monitor somewhere. Electronic notes don't work for this—it has to be real paper and stuck in your line of vision. Then I invite them every time they are thinking about something, or struggling to say no, to look at the Post-it and think of me saying to them, "Just stop it."

I shared this technique with a client, an executive who was leaving his job as a divisional president to go to another division. His peers kept asking his advice on more and more projects and business development ideas because they were going to miss his input when he moved on. He didn't like saying no to helping them, but he wanted to because it was overwhelming him as he was trying to learn his new job and detach from his old job. He greeted my Post-it idea with the typical eye rolling. But he humored me and tried it, and it wasn't long before I got a text from him with a photo of the Post-it note, telling me about the request he had just said no to. He was absolutely delighted, and it started a new trend for him—being ruthless, in a thoughtful way about what he would say no to.

Whenever you're wondering whether you should be more ruthless and say no, chances are you really do need to say no. Not everyone needs the visual reminder of Post-it with "Just stop it," but many do. Some clients call me and say, "Val, I know I should say no to this, but what do you think?" As you build your new muscle memory for saying no, sometimes you may need that kind of outside validation, letting you know that it's okay to say no. One great way to build accountability into making this change is to find a peer who is good at saying no and ask them whether they will help you if you get caught saying yes too much.

Once you practice this more, you will quiet the voices in your head until they become a whisper.

THE IMMEDIACY EFFECT

Tasks are like dust balls—the more you let them roll around the place, the larger they get. When you start and stop a task repeatedly, as we explore in Chapter 6, you expend parallel repetitive time and energy on it, so the faster you can start and finish a task, the more productive you will be.

Many executives' calendars look like a box of spilled jigsaw puzzle pieces. It is common for many to be double or triple booked, and so they rightly ask me, "When am I meant to get my actual work done, Val?" This is where the immediacy effect kicks in. First, you have to say no to a standard meeting. You do this by booking 15-, 30-, or 45-minute meetings. This is alien to many corporations. Shortly after a games company had been acquired, I remember their head designer saying to me, "Val, why does every decision take precisely 60 minutes? Even if we have made a decision in minute number 22, we still keep talking for a further 38 minutes." I was amused by the brilliance of this observation. Unfortunately, when you are in the depths of corporate norms, you don't notice such patterns, but to a creative games designer, it was as obvious as where the next key was to unlock the gate to the next level in their game.

One efficient way to take charge of the time that meetings consume (and the work that they generate) is to start the meeting by saying you need to end the meeting 10 minutes early. Stick to it, and then use that 10 minutes to act on what you learned in the meeting. It is too easy to spend the whole day going to meetings and collecting actions along the way, so you end the day with another day's work in your pocket. The trick is to act immediately and fast so you are not gathering additional work. If you are able to do this in five meetings a day, that gives you 50 minutes each day, or over four hours a week, of actual working time to get your tasks completed.

The immediacy effect also works with how you respond to questions, your in-box, and requests for help. You need to reply immediately. Many people hold off replying because they want to think, consider, and give a thoughtful response. But these are the times to be more ruthless, not more thoughtful. Most people only read the first line of an e-mail and then scan the rest; yet, sometimes when we write an e-mail, we spend a lot of time crafting it. That is not time well spent. When our answer to a request is yes, it is easy to fire that off quickly. But when we want to respond with a no, we often put that off—or we say yes when we want to say no. In fact, we can just as quickly write an e-mail reply saying no, but we often feel the need to justify and explain ourselves when all that is required is a simple no.

There are two areas where this issue is most common—when being introduced to someone new and in hiring. I have been guilty in the past of making poor introductions. A perfect introduction should be after both parties have agreed they want to be connected. Then when you finally make the introduction, it is welcomed. But if you forget to make a qualified introduction, it makes it hard (but not impossible!) to say no thanks when someone asks to meet you. Chapter 8 explores how to perfect your connections, but when you need to say no, you will free up more time if you say no straightaway. Otherwise, the inevitable happens: You get follow-up calls or e-mails, each one a little more persistent, until finally you may cave and agree to meet when you don't want to, or you may enter into correspondence that is further wasting your time. All of which could have been avoided if you had simply said "no thank you" at the time.

The second example is with hiring. The number one complaint I hear from executives seeking their next move is that nobody tells them no, and they would rather be told no than have complete radio silence. At Amazon, we attempted to tackle this issue because we had so many candidates in the system at any time and so many divisions competing for the same talent. In the fashion business, we introduced a simple tagging system in which managers were allowed to tag a candidate for their role, but they had just two weeks to make a decision if they wanted them; if they didn't, they had to decline and allow the candidate to be passed onto the next group. This simple step allowed the candidates to get interviews or rejection letters faster, and it forced managers to make quicker decisions if they wanted to interview a buyer or a merchandiser for their team before the next team got to look at them. You can speed decisions in your organization by creating systems that allow no to be easily decided and communicated.

Another side to the immediacy effect is apparent when you consider how you self-filter what you want to say and do. You say no to yourself before the words have gone from your brain to your mouth. You can tell if this is true for you by thinking back to a time when you were going to quit your job, but you hadn't yet told anyone at work—not your boss, your company, or your board. In that interim period of time, something has shifted in your head when you know you are leaving and nobody else does. I call this the pre-quit-power-zone, because knowing you will soon be out the door usually provides people with an explosion of power, confidence, and authority to say no without any perceived consequences.

An executive recently shared with me that in the weeks before she finally handed in her resignation she stopped pulling all-nighters to prepare for board presentations, shut down her voice of self-doubt, and started saying what she really thought about the company strategy. She was overwhelmed with the positive reaction and said she wished she had changed her behavior years ago. She figured she would have tripled her earning potential with the faster promotions and larger bonuses that she would have received.

When you are in the pre-quit-power-zone, suddenly you find yourself giving feedback that you've previously withheld to your peers, telling the truth about misguided strategy, and offering your team parting words of wisdom about what they should do with their careers and lives. If you could quiet the voice in your head that tells you no and filters your actions, harnessing that power for yourself and your team without actually quitting your job, imagine the results you would see.

The final area in which the immediate effect shows up is in how you either make or avoid a decision after expending effort. Imagine you are shopping for a new gadget: How long would you typically spend researching, comparing, considering, and debating? Do you ultimately purchase the item or say to yourself, "No, I am not going to buy that yet, or not from this retailer." This is where a no can hurt you when the consequences of a yes are minuscule. Back to your purchase: Is it a significant amount or an insignificant amount? I know leaders who spend hours researching which $100 bike rack to buy or which pair of headphones they want when a fast decision would be inconsequential. Researching vacations, hotel bookings, flight choices, or home improvement tools, and saying, "No, not right now," or "No, not at this price," are also a waste of your time. Quite simply the 10 percent variance on the $50 price tag is not worth your additional hour of time researching, so stop saying no and get to a decision faster to free up your time.

HOW TO BE PRODUCTIVELY UNPRODUCTIVE

It is a fallacy that you have to be productive every minute of your waking hour. Once you have control on how thoughtfully ruthless you are with your time and you are planning and prioritizing effectively, a little bit of procrastination actually is a fun way to spend your day. But you need to learn to be productively unproductive.

There are three rules to being productively unproductive. If these conditions are met, then you can give yourself permission to be unproductive:

1. You have achieved your stated goals for the day.
2. You pick something from your *productively unproductive* list.
3. You do not allow yourself to feel guilty or regretful for making an unproductive choice.

The challenge with being unproductive is that many people do it when they have a big deadline looming or they are avoiding a particular task. But if you build time into your workweek wherein you have the flexibility to be unproductive, then it takes all the stress away.

Always have handy a list of procrastination tasks. The tasks need to be things that can be accomplished relatively quickly and can't be time sensitive—tasks that need doing but not immediately. Then, when you are sitting down to write that report or create something new and you are not quite ready, you can give yourself a 15-minute procrastination break. But instead of checking out your favorite news sites or messaging your friends, pick a procrastination task from your list and feel proud that you are being productively unproductive.

HOW TO CONTROL INPUT OVERLOAD

One fast way to improve your power of no is to control your input. Now with so many devices, messaging apps, and ways to be contacted, it is important to have many tools at hand to keep the input at a minimum and in control. Here are some of the most powerful ways:

Delete All of Your E-Mail

Listen to any returning executive after vacation and you will hear them complain about the size of their in-box upon their return. J. Allard, corporate vice president of the Entertainment Division at Microsoft, had a brilliant solution to that. When he returned, he just deleted everything—yes, everything, as in select-all-delete-confirm-yes-permanently-delete. He used to go around with a great big grin on his face when he returned from his latest snowboard adventures because he never came back overwhelmed. He started a trend at Xbox. Many followed in his footsteps, perhaps with a slightly more cautious approach by setting an e-mail auto response telling people they were on vacation and on return they would be deleting their e-mail so please resend after a particular date. This set a new acceptable norm, and this was 10 years ago when the proliferation of many messaging apps had yet to take over.

Teach People How to Interact with You

Successful leaders train their team and peers how to interact with them. Don't like e-mail? Only want to talk by phone? Love one-page summaries? Hate long e-mails? Want open space in meetings? Or love minute-by-minute agendas? Let people know. Whatever your preference, the most effective way thoughtfully ruthless leaders prevent themselves from having to say no all the time and prevent themselves from being overloaded is by training those around them how to interact with them.

The best time to do this is when you first join a team. You are still in your honeymoon period and everyone is open to getting to know you and learning new ways of working. If you aren't in a new role, it isn't too late, but it will require some education.

I worked with a regional retail manager who had trained his store managers perfectly. He wanted a one-page summary of store performance in his in-box by 10 AM every Monday. He also explained the level of detail and information and format that he expected. When a new store manager joined from another region, the regional manager forgot to tell that manager how he liked to receive information. In one week, he had more than 35 e-mails from the new manager, and he was frustrated. After he spoke to his store manager, he learned that his previous regional manager was a slight control freak and wanted daily sales reports as well as e-mails if there were any positive or negative anomalies, along with a breakdown level of detail on every brand in the store. Once the regional manager had reset the store manager's expectations, he no longer received 35 e-mails a week from him. This was a simple issue to resolve, but these miscommunications of expectations happen all the time.

I worked with one leader who sent this e-mail out to his team:

Dear: Team
From: President
Subject: Thank you

Please take this e-mail as a worldwide thank you from everyone to everyone else. Now I have sent this e-mail, please nobody ever send an e-mail of thanks again about a simple receipt of an e-mail.

Regards,
President

This might seem a little harsh and a little too ruthless, but he counted his e-mails, and one day he had 75 e-mails whose sole purpose was to say thank you. It was completely unnecessary input overload. True to his request, nobody sent unnecessary thank-you e-mails again, and his input overload was reduced.

How is excessive e-mail or messaging causing you and others in your organization to be overwhelmed, and how could you remove it?

YOUR LOST DISCIPLINE LIST

By now you may becoming aware about what causes you to lose your discipline. Can you quickly name the top three reasons why you don't achieve what you planned to? Some people can quickly come up with the reasons, others need time to reflect to figure it out, and others need to talk to a trusted advisor or mentor to identify the root cause of what is happening. This is worth taking time to consider and understand, because there is one crucial element that sets apart exceptional leaders: discipline.

Knowing how to accelerate your discipline and being conscious of the triggers that cause you to lose it can transform your results and your reputation. If you do not identify your *lost discipline list,* you will waste all of your time setting goals and creating plans, because you need to know what causes you to lose your discipline so you can address it and stay on track.

Take time now to reflect and list what causes you to lose your discipline. Try to name at least five things.

If you don't know why, think about your goals from 12 months ago. How many did you meet, miss, or exceed? What caused you to miss goals?

If you can't immediately identify what caused you to miss those goals, apply the *toddler why test* by asking yourself why, why, why, but why? until you get to the root cause of what is getting in your way.

You may want to review your lost discipline list with someone you trust and can have a candid conversation with so you can be sure you are identifying the true root causes of your lost discipline. I often lose my discipline if I am tired or have not been exercising. Also if I am trying something new for the first time, I may take longer than normal and allow myself to get distracted rather than just focus on what I am trying to do.

Once you know your top three causes, you can address them and get on with setting goals that you can actually achieve and exceed. This is preferable to lofty resolutions that will be forgotten a month later.

If you are in the top 5 percent of exceptional performers who always exceed what they set out to achieve, make sure you know the factors that accelerate your discipline so you can replicate your success. See Chapter 7 for an in-depth discussion of accelerators.

The Toughest Person to Say No To

The hardest person to say no to is to yourself. Stopping procrastination is the ultimate test of saying no to yourself. Many lost discipline lists I see from executives are full of electronic distractions—websites, social media, e-mail, or the latest instant messaging service. These things can easily distract you as you try to work on your laptop. There is a technical solution to this technical problem, and I'm not talking about the apps you can get that switch off your social media channels when you focus. My suggestion is that you get an air-gapped laptop. I learned about this from an episode of *The Newsroom*. A true air gap is when a computer is not physically connected to the Internet, and the only way to transfer information from and to it is with a USB drive. This inspired me to experiment with this idea for myself because this physical barrier is the precise barrier sometimes needed to avoid distraction.

If simply switching off your Wi-Fi isn't barrier enough for your distractions, perhaps a dedicated computer for focused work could work for you. I wrote a large portion of this book on an air-gapped Mac. Well, it was not a totally air-gapped Mac, because I could access my Dropbox account, but I didn't have any of my e-mail or other distracting links and apps to capture my attention. In doing so, I tripled my writing productivity in one day, so I tried testing it with my clients, and they found it helped them to get creating, writing, or thinking done in less time.

Saying no to yourself—and to procrastination—can be hard work, but the payoff is big. Do what you need to do to make the most of your work time so you can make the most of your personal time.

THIRTY WAYS TO SAY NO

Getting language right is like learning a new sport—you have to practice in order to make it second nature. Learning to say no is much like learning a new language. To learn to say no more often, you need to understand there are three varieties of no, because no does not always mean no. When you say no, you may mean not right now, you may mean not that way, or you really may mean no.

Here are some clear phrases for any situation.

No! Not Now, Not Ever

1. I am not available then.
2. I cannot give that the attention it deserves.
3. That will not work for me.
4. Thanks for the offer, but I have to decline.

5. No, thank you.
6. That is not possible.
7. I cannot say yes to that.
8. I would rather not.
9. I am already focused on ABC.
10. I can't.
11. It sounds wonderful, but I have to say no.
12. Thank you for asking, but I need to decline.
13. It's absolutely not possible.

Not Now, but Another Time

1. That could work if it can be in June, but not this month.
2. If it is important that I attend, let's plan for next week.
3. I would love to attend, but I cannot make that date.
4. It is not a priority for me right now.
5. I have other priorities I have to put first.
6. I cannot do that until October, but a member of my team could sooner.
7. I would love to meet you, but until my product launches, that needs to be my priority. Let's get back in touch after November.
8. I am not prioritizing that right now, but next year perhaps.
9. I have made a commitment to x for the next month. Perhaps next month?

Not That Way, but My Way

1. If your goal is this, how about we approach it this way?
2. Why did you choose that way? Are you open to other ideas?
3. I could say yes if you are open to approaching it a different way.
4. If you explain why that is your solution, I will explain an alternative.
5. My experience tells me that won't work, have you considered . . .
6. I don't want to do it that way. Can we try this instead?
7. I am interested, but I want to do it my way, is that an option?
8. I agree with what you want to do, but I want to change how it's done. Is that possible?

WARNING: Worst Phrases to Say When You Mean No and You Want to Say No

1. Yes.
2. I will consider it.

3. Perhaps
4. Let me think about it.
5. Interesting . . .
6. Maybe.
7. Let's talk about it.

Not using any phrases and simply remaining silent is also a bad choice. In the absence of words, your silence will sound a lot like yes.

Most of us don't say no enough because it can be so hard to say. It is hoped you now feel more empowered to say no whenever you need to. I have found that saying no is the only way to say yes to the things I want to say yes to.

Here are a few final tips that should make it easier for you to say the nos you need to say:

- Say no as soon as you know you don't want to do or can't do something. Delaying it wastes energy and decreases the likelihood of alternatives.
- Use a presumptive close. Don't ask a question such as "Shall we meet next week?" Instead, say, "Let's meet on Wednesday."
- It is easier to say no and then change your answer to yes than it is to say yes and then have to say no. If you are unsure about your answer or availability, say no.

Chapter 6

SHUSH!

How to Create Silence, Space, and Time

The first time someone on my team told me to shush, I was stunned. She had the desired effect, however; I was quiet, for at least long enough to ask her, why did you tell me to shush? I soon found out that she would regularly say, "Shush!" to her peers and executives. While her tone may have bristled a few, her intent was clear. She needed silence to think, to reflect, or just to get a word in between many energetic and boisterous leaders. I led a dynamic group of leaders, driving change and leadership improvements across an IT consulting firm, so we were no quiet bunch. We were running fast, making acquisitions, and hiring rapidly, and I was failing as their leader because I was not creating the most readily available and free resource for my team: silence and space.

YOUR DAILY SILENCE

Now that you have your *sensible selfish charter* and your newfound ability to say no, you need the freedom to give you and your team the gift of silence. I am not suggesting you go and tell your team or boss to shush, but you can give your team the perfect gift of silence and space. In this noisy world of endless tweets, likes, shares, pins, and posts, many leaders I work with tell me they are overwhelmed and don't prioritize time to think, to reflect, and to focus on the future. For that you need silence. To achieve it, you'll need to be a little more thoughtful and a lot more ruthless with creating and protecting time for reflection.

Bill Gates created Think Week at Microsoft to allow him a week at the beach each year with 300 ideas from around the company for him to comment on and respond to. Originally, this would be Bill lugging boxes of papers to his beach hideaway to think and reflect, then it evolved to including the top 50 technical experts across Microsoft to take the time and space to reflect and think about the possibilities of the future. Richard Branson creates similar silence and space for entrepreneurs on his private British Virgin Island retreats. The good news is you don't have to rent an island to build silence into your week; follow the Nine Steps to Silence Guide to give you and your team just what you need:

Nine Ways to Create Silence
1. Start with you.

Book silence sessions in your calendar and protect them ruthlessly from cancellation. Schedule these sessions during your regular working hours—don't count Saturday mornings! Carve out a new routine, stick to it, and tell others why it is valuable for you.

2. Schedule fake meetings.

You can't do this too often without getting found out. Book a meeting for three hours, at the start of the day. The day before the meeting, cancel it with this message to your team: "I am giving you this gift of three hours. Use it wisely to think, reflect, and plan. If this isn't your ideal thinking time, go walk your dog, do some personal chores, and schedule your own silence session later this week at your perfect thinking time." Your team will thank you for it.

3. Create silence sessions in meetings.

Who is the first to speak in your team meetings? If it is always you, then you are missing out on hearing what your team really thinks. If it is always one or two particular people, then they are unfairly dominating decisions, strategy, and opinions. Control the flow and participants in meetings; if you are the one always dominating, ask your team to notice and let you know.

4. Silence in the car.

Instead of queuing up two podcasts or listening to NPR during your next commute, try driving in silence. While music can be relaxing, silence can give your brain permission to wander wherever it wants to rather than being forced to follow a strict path, subject to your own personal satellite navigation system. Try switching off all of the information, music, and distractions on your next drive and let your mind wander in peace. See where the silence takes you.

5. Start and end every business trip alone.

It is tempting to book your business trips to minimize your time away from the office, when you should do the complete reverse. Start your trip with a quiet meal alone to plan what you want to achieve and what impression you want to leave. Then end your trip with quiet reflection. Time to decompress is critical. Even if it is just for a cup of coffee, give yourself the gift of silence to reflect, to capture your thoughts, and to decide what was successful and how you can replicate that success.

6. Ask permission to think for a moment.

I used to work with a leader who would regularly say, "Let's take a 10-minute break," right at a crucial point in his executive team meeting. It was usually when a decision was about to be made about an acquisition or we were just reaching a conclusion on investing in a new initiative. When I asked him why, he told me it was because he needed silence and time to think because the heat of the moment was sometimes too overwhelming. During the break, he would go for a walk and collect his thoughts in silence; he would then return to the executive discussion prepared. Instead of mentally kicking yourself after a meeting for all of the possible points you could have made, ask for a short recess and take your own silence break.

7. Listen to the silence.

Unless you regularly practice yoga, meditate, or already prioritize alone time, silence may seem unusual—and even uncomfortable—at first. You may have a ringing in your ears or have multiple ideas or thoughts racing through your head at once. Write them down, acknowledge them, and listen to the silence.

8. Be a little bit random.

Don't be overly structured and prescriptive. Sometimes your brain needs to think messy. I have five-year-old twins and a seven-year-old.

Whenever my husband or I take one out for some alone time, their conversations are crazy. They love the space that having one-on-one time gives them, and they fill it with stories, ideas, and questions, barely remembering to breathe between each. Give your brain some unscripted silence and see where it takes you.

9. Book a recurring meeting with yourself.

Silence cannot be a onetime event that you retreat to in times of high stress or during vacations. Habits form when we replace old triggers with new triggers. Give yourself permission to go to your favorite lunch spot with a spectacular view once a month. Schedule an appointment with yourself and ruthlessly protect that time.

Once you practice these silence habits, you'll soon realize how deafening the rest of your life is. Just like when you first try a new challenging sport, you will need to practice this repeatedly before it becomes second nature. Once you begin to truly appreciate silence, you can begin to understand the power of the gift of time.

THE GIFT OF TIME

Have you ever sat down at 8 PM on a Sunday evening and wondered what happened to the weekend? Time doesn't truly fly, but if you are not ruthlessly paying attention, you can miss minutes, days, weeks, and years. Facebook has just introduced a new feature called *memories*, where you can look back on your photos and commentary from previous years. While it is a wonderful feature to look back on photos lost in cyberspace, it does prompt many questions about where the time has gone. The challenge is not how to slow down time because no one can do that. The challenge is how to make the most of every hour so you are intentionally focusing on what matters do you.

We regularly tell ourselves that we don't have enough time when we actually do. You just are choosing to spend it in different places. Time management isn't about finding more time; it's about being thoughtfully ruthless with where you do spend your time and how you stop more than how you start. How you prioritize your time and where you choose not to do things is almost more important than what you choose to do. You may already know where you could reprioritize your time; if not, you may need to reflect.

Daily Procrastination Destination Minutes	Minutes per Year	Hours per Year	Hours Saved	Days Saved
15	5,475	91	65	8
30	10,950	183	130	16
60	21,900	365	261	33
120	43,800	730	521	65

If you spend 15 minutes per day at your procrastination destination, that is 5,475 minutes every year; or 91 hours

If you didn't visit your procrastication destination just Monday through Friday you would free up 65 hours a year, which equates to eight free days to use as you choose

Figure 6.1 Spending Less Time on Procrastination Destinations

Here is a quick exercise: Spending time on online on news websites and social media is one of the top procrastination destinations I hear from executives and entrepreneurs. Think about how much time you spend online in a typical day. Now imagine for a minute if you reduced that by just 15 minutes a day. Doing so Monday through Friday, every week for a year, would save 65 hours, which is actually the equivalent of eight days. You have the power to give yourself back the gift of eight days a year, more if you can cut out 30 or 60 minutes a day. Looking at how your time can add up may cause you to prioritize your time differently (see Figure 6.1).

You may not use social media to procrastinate. Your procrastination destination may be something else, but think about where you are spending time that you could cut out. Which meetings are taking unnecessary time? Which distractions are you getting absorbed by? How could you make some changes? Remember the cycle of awareness and change of behavior: first you have to be aware and then you have to commit to making those changes.

I've tried this myself. I used to spend time on social media sites, including Facebook and Twitter, 30 minutes every day, 5 minutes here, 5 minutes there. For three weeks, I cut out checking any social media Monday through Friday, and I deleted my apps off my phone to give me even more discipline. Studies show that multitasking prevents fast focus, so the more you can remove distractions, the faster you will increase your productivity. I found myself more focused, less distracted, and actually got things finished faster so I could go off and do something for me at the end of the day like go for a run or read a book, which is far more rewarding than sporadic dabbling on Twitter and Facebook!

It's relatively easy to let hours and days slip away from focus without clear goals every day. Many companies spend weeks and months perfecting annual goals and long-term strategies, but the fastest way to make immediate progress is to set specific daily goals for yourself. This is the critical first step of every productive day. Complete this fast exercise to understand where you can give yourself the gift of time:

Your Achievement Rate

1. At the start of your day, write down what you will accomplish.
2. At the end of every day, record what you accomplished as well as your insights into your day.
3. After two weeks, take a look at what patterns have emerged that you can address and ask yourself these questions:
   - Do you always achieve what you say you will?
   - What distracts you from achieving your goals?
   - What do you need to change to improve your achievement rate?

You can also ask your team to complete this exercise and ask them how you can help them improve their achievement rate.

Being thoughtfully ruthless with your time is not just about achieving goals. Another aspect is about whether you are working on the right work, so you need to identify if you and your team are focused on the right spot.

Focus on the Right Spot

Fewer than 10 percent of executives tell me they have the perfect balance of where they are spending their time. The other 90 percent don't feel like they are spending enough time on longer-term strategic areas of their business. Take a look at Figure 6.2. It is my most popular visual that I draw for executives. Start by reflecting on the last three months of your work: Ask yourself where your time and energy has been focused. Has it been on customers, products, and finances of the immediate here and now? Has it been on projects and initiatives that will impact your business in three to six months time? Or has it been on your two- or three-year growth plan? Plot yourself on the horizontal axis on the Focus on the Right Spot chart.

Now reflect on the type of work you have been engaged in. Have you been executing, planning, considering strategic choices, or engaged in complete blue-sky thinking? Plot yourself on the vertical axis below. Take a look at where you sit on the chart. Are you in the right zone for your role?

This is how I have discovered that only 10 percent of executives are actually focused on the right spot. There is such a strong gravitational pull to the bottom left-hand corner that it takes extreme focus and discipline to stay in the right zone, whether you are a board member, a CEO, or a leader.

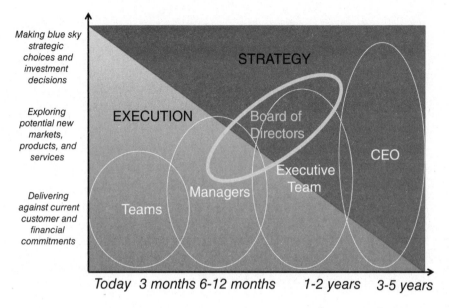

Figure 6.2 Focusing in the Right Spot

If you are in the wrong spot, ask yourself why? Are you failing to delegate? Do you not have the right leadership team in place so you are diving in too deep? Do you need to remind your team when to make decisions themselves versus when they need to bring you in (see Figure 6.2)?

Now let's look at some more techniques the most effective leaders use to be intentional with where they spend their time.

IN-BOX IN CONTROL

Do you remember when your in-box was a physical tray? Your input for work involved a knock at the door, a paper letter, your desk phone ringing, or some verbal direction from a meeting you attended. Compare that to today when your virtual in-box consists of your e-mail in-box; texts; phone calls; Skype messages; incoming FaceTime; WhatsApp/Slack/Zoom messages; notifications on LinkedIn, Instagram, and Pinterest; and tweets and direct messages on Twitter. The list is endless, and by the time this book is published, it will probably be completely out of date!

There are some leaders who calmly and systematically review and respond to their e-mail, but many are overwhelmed. Like a hamster on a wheel, they feel like they are always running to catch up. Subscriptions, notifications from social media, and "must click" offers clutter many in-boxes, when really you only want to hear from your customers and employees. While there are many productivity tools that claim to stream-line your electronic e-mail, you don't need technology to fix technology, you need organization and discipline.

I was working with an organization of a large technology company and they said their number one barrier that slowed down their ability to innovate was the volume and frequency of e-mail. Long repetitive threads would multiply exponentially. While companies in France have instilled rules that prevent e-mail from being sent outside of office hours (including weekends), we have no such rules here in the states. Without such rules, how do you get your in-box back in control? Here are my best tips for doing just that.

Eleven Ways to Control Your In-Box

The Opener

Having an action decision or an FYI in the subject header really helps people prioritize. Then make sure your first sentence is clear and action oriented. Ask the question in the first sentence. State the purpose of the e-mail in the first sentence. Be concise. Why use a paragraph when a sentence will do? Why use a sentence when a word will do? I find many leaders send really long, rambling e-mails when it's not necessary. Get to the point.

Take Your Time

The first step to in-box organization is blocking time on your calendar to tackle your current in-box and set up a new system of organization. During this housekeeping, clear out your in-box. You don't have to delete it, but move it out of the way. Set up a folder with today's date, and get rid of it all. This will allow you to start fresh tomorrow with a new discipline.

Use Auto-Signatures

I learned this from a buyer at Amazon. She told me that every click on your keyboard is precious. There is a way to shortcut commonly used phrases and responses by using the auto signature feature. What questions do you get repeatedly? What information do you regularly send out? Create a series of auto signatures so that with one click you can insert links, quotes, or sentences. You can create your own fast response system.

Only Let in Customers, Employees, and Investors

I am fascinated when I peep into executives' in-boxes; those who willingly share are those who use their e-mail to their advantage and don't allow themselves to be suffocated by it. Those in control have rules and folders organized meticulously. Go old-school and grab a pencil and paper and draw out buckets of e-mails that you want organized either by sender or by topic with the goal of getting everything out of your in-box apart from your customers, employees, and investors.

Create rules for all subscriptions and social media alerts, and send them to a separate folder. Create one folder called *an in-box organized* with subfolders like Alerts, Subscriptions, Promotions, and key people you want flagged quickly. It makes it easier to hide these noncritical e-mail folders and prevents distraction. When only your customers and employees are in your main in-box, you can give them the priority they deserve and reduce your distractions.

Make It a Team Effort

You may think this will never work, that your circumstances and your team is different, but try it anyway. Make taming the in-box a team effort. You will have to do some education and as a leader influence your peers and boss, but you have an opportunity to create some change. Here's a suggestion of what you can send to your team to help them manage their in-box as well (see Figure 6.3).

This is an e-mail I have adapted from ones I have seen work when you are trying to make changes in how e-mail is handled within teams. Adapt it and send it to your team and peers.

Don't Dump Your To-Do List

One of the greatest fallacies I hear about e-mail management is this: "I may send e-mail at 9 PM, but I don't expect a response." This is misguided because of course your employees are going to read it—and because you're their boss, they'll probably respond because they think they should. You don't need to send it. If it's not business critical and it's not going to affect customers or product profits in the next 24 hours, wait until the morning. Send it on the auto-delay or put it in your drafts. Sending nonurgent e-mail late at night is like dumping your to-do list on someone else and asking them not to read it or respond.

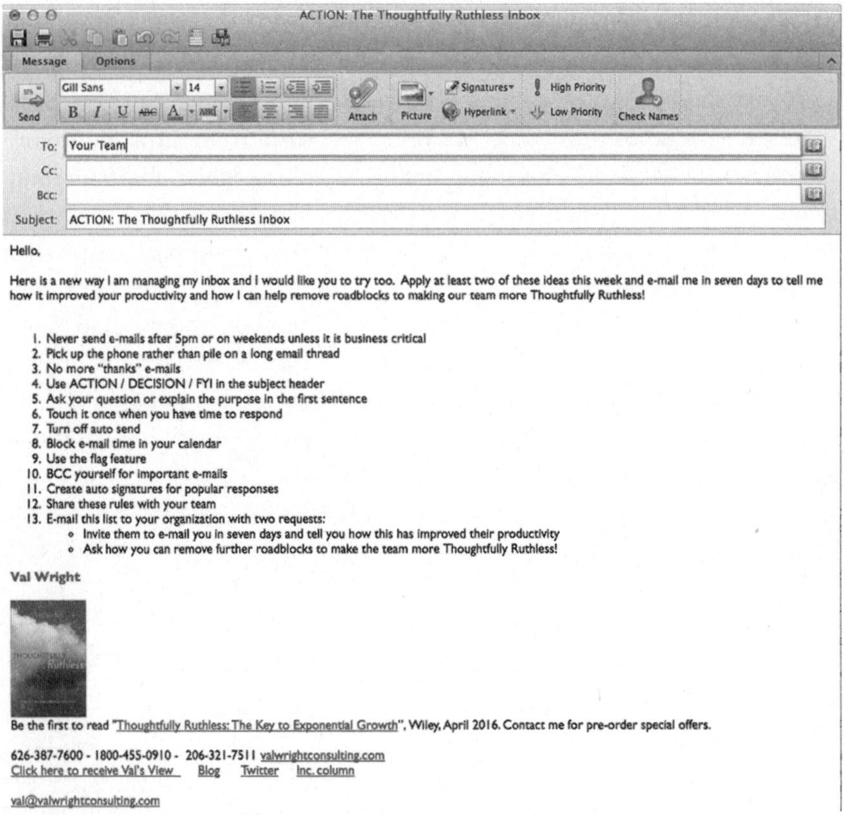

Figure 6.3 Changing How E-Mail Is Handled

© Val Wright Consulting. All rights reserved.

Try the Phone

Although it may seem that technology has made phones obsolete, one five-minute phone call can sometimes replace 30 e-mails. If it is during regular business hours, and there's opportunity to pick up the phone rather than add to a long e-mail list, do it.

Stop Saying Thank You

Having the power to say no to the types of e-mails you receive and send will get your in-box in control. What are your greatest e-mail annoyances? Share them with your team and set a new standard for what you expect. How can you reduce the volume of unnecessary e-mails? My worst is the e-mails that simply say "Thanks!"

Incessant Knock at the Door

Could you imagine sitting in your office and allowing people to knock on your door every 30 seconds? Probably not, but many of us allow its virtual equivalent by permitting e-mail notifications to pop up visually on your screen, or vibrate or ding on your phone, watch, or tablet. Turn off auto-sync, and schedule time in your calendar to respond to e-mail when that will be your sole focus. Only touch the e-mail once, open it, and respond to it and be done with it. This is much more efficient than constantly monitoring your e-mail, fiddling with it while you're walking into meetings, but not actually respond to it and then going back to it. Be deliberate about how you spend your time.

Use the Online/Offline Mode

Avoid distractions from your e-mail by switching to offline mode. Schedule specific times of the day to check and respond to e-mail so it doesn't take over your life. Regularly put your phone in airplane mode and leave it in a different part of your office (rather than permanently attached to your hand) to prevent the temptation to check it constantly.

Don't Open It Unless You Are Going to Respond

The greatest e-mail time suck is touching an e-mail multiple times. Mindlessly checking your e-mail on your phone when you don't have the ability to immediately craft a response creates double the work.

Once you have mastered the *11 factors for thoughtfully ruthless e-mail*, you will improve your own productivity, but your greatest opportunity is getting your team and peers to adopt the *thoughtfully ruthless e-mail factors*. Don't forget to use the sample e-mail in Figure 6.3 to share with your team your expectations for how e-mail and online messaging works in your organization.

CALENDAR CHAOS

Not surprisingly, effectively managing your calendar is a critical way to give yourself the gift of time. Do these eight common mistakes managing the calendar sound familiar to you?

1. Your calendar spawns a life of its own. It is easy for meetings to creep onto your calendar when you don't know their purpose, don't accept

a request just to talk, or catch up, don't accept reoccurring meetings, and regularly cull your calendar for meetings that just have grown into your regular calendar.

2. Failing to say no to meetings. Stop automatically accepting every meeting. Ask what the purpose is and question whether you need to attend personally or can delegate it to someone on your team.

3. Don't delegate appropriately. Ask your team to give you feedback about the meetings they attend. Ask whether you should have shown up to meetings that you had declined.

4. Disconnected from your core priorities. Go back to your ideal percentage mix of time. Are you driving your core priorities or are you actually spending your time differently than you intend? Track your time over a two-week period and compare it to where you ideally want to be spending your time; make adjustments accordingly.

5. Forget to reset after changes. After a recent promotion, a new product line, or a change in focus, you have to press reset on where you are spending your time. Do a quarterly clean-up of your calendar to refresh where you are spending your time.

6. Ignore the power of the executive admin. If I want to find out how thoughtfully ruthless you are, ask your executive admin. They manage your calendar and have the greatest insight into your calendar.

7. Fail to schedule your to-do list. Schedule your to-do list into your calendar. If you don't have dedicated time to complete a task, it is far less likely to get done. I often sit down with leaders and ask them to see their to-do lists. It's usually 50 lines long, and when I ask how many things have been on there for over three weeks, it is usually more than half, which means they're probably not big priorities. Unless you put your to-do list into your calendar and schedule time for action, it's highly unlikely to happen—or you will end up doing it in obscure hours of the day, after all your meetings are finished.

8. Lack a thoughtfully ruthless calendar plan. I recommend having a thoughtfully ruthless calendar with a "my choice" hour of the day. You do this by making the last hour of your day blocked and open for you to do as you choose. Don't schedule your day with meetings right up until the minute you are due out of the door. Instead, spend the last hour working on things you want to work on versus rushing from your final meeting as you remember that you have yet to answer three important e-mails or you still have work to do on that deadline.

Your Thoughtfully Ruthless Calendar

Sometimes we get so stuck in the way we've always done things that it's difficult to even think of new ways to approach our time. Use this exercise to unlock the possibilities. The idea is to dream of what it would be like if you were in complete control of your time and how you would ideally approach your work and life:

> Design your ideal day:
> Include start time, finish time, and approach to personal commitments.
> Design your ideal week:
> Include remote working, approach to weekends, and so forth.
> Design your ideal year:
> Include ideal number and frequency of vacations, long weekends, amount of business travel, and so forth.
> Design your ideal allocation of time:
> What would be your ideal allocation of work by percentage?

Now examine how you currently spend your day, week, and year. Knowing the gap between the two is the first step to making changes that will make you more thoughtfully ruthless.

Figure 6.4 shows what an ideal calendar can look like. Consider how you can block in chunks of time to review projects, plan for inspiring communication, dedicate time to the future stars of your organization, and leave time available for open space and spontaneous conversations.

A crucial part of getting your calendar under control is how you manage and plan meetings. Making meetings meaningful will catapult how effective you and your organization are, so that's what we'll look at next.

MEANINGFUL MEETINGS

I used to work at the Rare Games Studio in England shortly after Microsoft acquired it for $375 million to make games for Xbox. Founded by three brothers, the studio was made up of 250 artists, musicians, animators, and developers. The strangest part about working at this games studio was that there were no planned meetings. For the first time in my career, I had a wide open calendar of white space. If a decision needed to be made, a handful of people would huddle, make the decision, and move on. Simple, fast, and effective. Though a little unnerving at first, this was incredibly

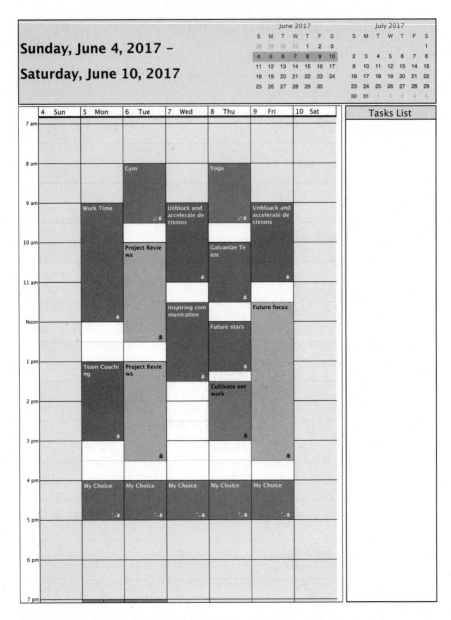

Figure 6.4 Your Thoughtfully Ruthless Calendar

freeing for me. My calendar was empty, and I could focus on doing work rather than talking about it.

While this may be an extreme that many can only dream about, you do have more control over your time than you think. I have sat in thousands of meetings; some have been effective and inspiring and others have made me want to run from the building screaming. If that is your situation, then you will probably be relieved to hear this: You can immediately reduce your investment in meetings by 75 percent. That's not a fantasy. Here is why: Half of all meetings are not needed. Those meetings that are needed require only half the attendees. The meetings that take place with half the people could be completed in at least half the time.

Picture your last meeting. If you were to add up the salary investment in employee time spent in meetings and then reduce it by 75 percent, what would your savings be? What if you redirected even half of this time to innovating new ways to offer value to your customers?

Companies and teams do not innovate in meetings. Meetings creep and expand like the roots of a bamboo plant. Before you know it they have taken over, locked themselves in, and are sucking life and energy from everything around them.

Surprisingly, your furniture matters when it comes to making meetings count. Pixar used to have an oval table in its main conference room, and over time everyone knew that Ed Catmull and the other Pixar executives sat in the middle of the oval and the more junior people sat at the ends. There were even cheap seats in a second tier around the edge of the table where people sat to observe but rarely participate. Over time, the dynamic of the conversation focused solely on the center of the table in a powerful inner circle, until one day Ed realized that the table was the greatest barrier to everyone participating. The table went out with the trash.

Picture your meeting rooms; how does your layout affect who participates? Participation matters. You need to always have the right voices in the room. As you plan a meeting, don't just select based on hierarchy. Be sure to invite your best designer, technical expert, or customer advocate to make sure all of the right voices are heard. Ego invites don't help. Meetings are not a spectator sport, so don't invite someone just to watch. This is where you can give the gift of time back to your team; the more you document action items and decisions and then send those meeting notes out, the fewer people you need in the actual room, because often people attend meetings so they don't miss out. If you were sharing the notes and the actions and doing more post-meeting communication, you could reduce the number of attendees in meetings.

As fast companies grow, it is easy to get stuck in old ways of making decisions, so regularly press reboot on any recurring meetings and free up time. Peter Deng, head of product for Instagram, did this when he first joined the company. He canceled every existing meeting and replaced them all with just one 30-minute meeting for rapid-fire removal of road-blocks. When you join a new company, it is sometimes hard to translate and understand the meeting rules. Just like board games require clear instructions to know how to play them, meetings require parameters, too. Often when faced with meeting with executives, employees are unsure how to behave: Can I disagree? Should I interrupt? Do your team a favor and let people know what to expect and what is acceptable beforehand; this information is especially helpful when new people join your team.

Knowing how and when decisions are made in meetings helps to eliminate confusion as well. Make it clear what decisions need to be made and who will make the final call. Most meetings consist of information sharing, which is a waste of time and can usually be accomplished outside of a meeting. Be clear on the point of every meeting. If there isn't one, cancel it. I was observing a meeting at a technology company, and everybody was debating and talking about a new product and a new initiative. The problem was that everybody in the room thought they were giving input, but the truth was the product had already been decided. The features had already been locked in, and the reason for the meeting was to inform the room, not debate it, but people in the room thought they were contributing. There was a complete disconnect. Be clear with people before you bring topics to a meeting about whether you want their input, whether you're just telling them and nothing's going to change, or whether you're looking for decisions.

Amazon starts every meeting with reading a written document they call a narrative. It is not sent out ahead of time, so everyone literally gets on the same page at the start of the meeting by reading in silence. Then, the discussion begins page by page, questioning data, assumptions, and results. This allows everyone to participate. Even when Jeff Bezos is present, everyone in the room asks questions and makes suggestions. This avoids a derailing conversation on slide 2 of a PowerPoint presentation. Can you start your meetings with quiet reading?

Meaningful Meetings Assessment

Use this meaningful meetings assessment to rate all of the meetings you currently attend. Start by making a list of all of your recurring meetings. Then, evaluate each according to the criteria and ratings presented here.

Six Meaningful Meetings Criteria

1. A clear purpose
2. Intentional attendees
3. Clarity about whether informing, deciding, or debating
4. Attendees have all the same information before decisions are made
5. Deliberate use of time
6. Documented action items and follow-up

Rate Each Meeting

1. Exemplary: Achieves purpose effectively; no room for improvement
2. Could do better: Is effective in parts but does not meet the six critical meaningful meetings criteria
3. Energy sapper: Not a good use of my time

Meeting	Owner	Attendees (number and roles)	Purpose	Frequency & Duration	Rating

Now you have assessed how meaningful the meetings you attend are, ask yourself these three questions:

1. How can I change the meetings I own so they achieve the six meaningful meetings criteria?

2. How can I influence other meeting owners to improve their meaningful meeting rating?

3. In the short term, what meetings should I decline or delegate to free up my time?

Use this meaningful meeting assessment in your next meeting. At the start of the meeting, share the six meaningful meeting criteria and let your attendees know you will ask them to rate the meeting at the end so you can get feedback about how to improve.

As you make these changes, track how many hours you free up as a result of introducing meaningful meetings. Then intentionally redirect that time to your customers or employees.

THE THOUGHTFULLY RUTHLESS DEADLINE TRACKER

The final area that impacts how you are thoughtfully ruthless with your time is how you and your team manage your work against deadlines. Imagine you have a deadline coming up in a couple of months. When would you start thinking about the work? And when might you start working on it? Mentally picture when you're going to start. Do you think about it a lot before you begin? Do you think in little parts? Then when do you actually start the work? Do you start the work in one block, finish it, and you're done?

Use the *thoughtfully ruthless deadline tracker* in Figure 6.5 to discover whether you're an early deliverer, steady achiever, spotty dabbler, or

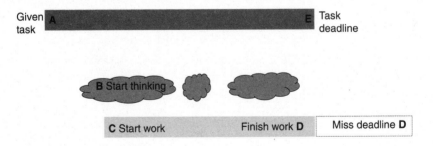

Figure 6.5   The Thoughtfully Ruthless Deadline Tracker
Point A: When you receive a deadline
Point B: When you first start thinking about the activity
Point C: When you first start action toward the activity
Point D: When you complete the activity
Point E: The deadline date

adrenaline addict. Understanding where you fall on the spectrum will help you learn how to unlock the ability to meet deadlines faster—with less stress and more fun.

Consider how you typically respond to deadlines by asking yourself these five questions:

1. How proactive are you in meeting deadlines?
2. How common is it for you to miss deadlines or forget you have one looming?
3. Do you prefer to think before taking action?
4. Do you iterate before moving forward?
5. Do you like to juggle multiple priorities or focus singularly and sequentially?

Your goal is to take the fastest, most effective route possible between the time when you receive a deadline and when you complete the activity (A–D).

Having studied this in corporations for over a quarter of a century, I have discovered there are four typical reactions to achieving deadlines:

Early Deliverer

In my corporate days, I had a boss who was an early deliverer and expected everyone on her team to be the same, except nobody told me that, and I wasn't clever enough to ask. I suffered one too many painful public chastising for being the last to complete a task, even though the deadline was weeks away. She even had someone on her team produce completion percentages (of which members of her leadership team had completed various tasks) on Excel graphs and published them regularly for the whole team to see. I never missed a deadline, but what I realized was that my manager did not value deadlines being simply met; they needed to be finished as fast as humanly possible once issued. I didn't last very long working for that manager before I decided to leave, but it did give me insight into what it is like working for an early deliverer when you are not typically one yourself.

Greatest dangers: First, check the results you are achieving and the feedback you are receiving, because there may be no real danger to early delivery. If you are an early deliverer, you may be in danger of skipping to the answer for the sake of ticking a box and completing a task. Build in extra time to make sure you are not being too ruthless with getting to the answer and perhaps build some more thoughtful reflection into what you are achieving.

Build on your strengths: Early deliverers are great at finding the fastest way to achieve a task and are regimented at knowing what deadlines have been issued and when they are due. If you manage a team, try teaming up an early deliverer with an adrenaline addict or a spotty dabbler, or give them responsibility for team tasks that require meticulous coordination and follow-up because they will get it done.

Spotty Dabbler

Many people do the think/do dance when working on a task. You think a little, you do a little. You think a little more, you do a little more. You may repeat that once or twice or multiple times, and then you stop, and then you think you do and you think you do, and then you stop. Spotty dabblers are most likely to miss a deadline because they are jumping between so many tasks it is hard to keep track. If you identify as sometimes a spotty dabbler, ask yourself why. When I first launched my consulting business, I wrote my first article that was two pages long. It took me 37 hours to write it. I was really proud I did it in 37 hours, really proud, and then I talked to some other people who told me they took 30 minutes to an hour, and I thought how can I possibly achieve that? I took my daughter's wind-up, blue owl timer that you crank (something I use when I try to get them to put on their pajamas at night without drama) and decided to treat myself like a 4-year-old. I wound it for 60 minutes, and I sat down. "I'm going to write my article." It took me 57 minutes, and I did it. Then I was just so excited. I started it again, and I wrote another one in 37 minutes, and then that was it. I knew I could do it faster. I had spent too long thinking and deliberating, but once I heard that others could do it faster, that was my motivation for trying to match that speed.

Greatest dangers: You are repeating unnecessary work, whether it is repetitive thinking or action, and it is a waste of time. Think about when you book a flight or a vacation, do you research, price, and make comparisons but don't commit and process the transaction? Next time, you come back to look again, prices may have changed, availability shifted, and so you have to repeat the effort to complete the task again. You may also be thinking about your decision while considering other work, which also is an energy suck. This interruption effect is a big distraction because each time you stop and start, you have to get back up to speed and repeat.

Build on your strengths: Consider how much of this time is productive think time versus what I call flitting in and out of a problem but not really focusing and applying correct energy to it (and then going from speaking about it to actually doing it). If this is your preferred way to think and act, getting organized will improve your efficiency. Intentionally chunk out your work so when you divide it up you make forward progress and do not repeat work.

Adrenaline Addict

I used to work with an executive who created remarkable work and was continually pushing his team, but the night before every board meeting or important presentation, you could guarantee he and his team would be at the office late working on the pitch, the materials, and the story. When I asked him about the regular pattern I observed, he said that he was running so fast he never had time to stop and plan so he could get ahead. And he said his team always delivered everything so late to him that he had no choice but to react at the 11th hour for every important deadline. He was an adrenaline addict and didn't really want to change. It wasn't until I showed him the effect he was having on his team that it became possible for him to escape the adrenaline trap with a little advance planning.

Greatest dangers: There are two dangers of continually leaving your deadlines until the last minute. First, you increase the probability that you will miss your deadline because you leave no capacity for other competing priorities that may take over. The second risk is that you don't produce your highest quality work because you are rushing and may be working late, tired, unable to gain feedback, or trying to complete three things at once — all of which may reduce the quality of your work.

Build on your strengths: Adrenaline addicts respond well under pressure, so they need deadlines and goals. If this is you, break your activities up into manageable chunks and set your own deadlines for achieving them. If this is someone on your team, ask them for their work ahead of the real date you need to build in buffer time. Working against a deadline eliminates fluff and pontification, it stops you from second-guessing, and you just get on and do it. Pay attention to your speed and results when that happens, because it proves that you have the capacity and capability to work at that pace again, so consider how you can replicate it.

Steady Achiever

The most structured are the steady achievers. They plan and achieve deadlines early. They schedule in tasks and always meet deadlines.

Greatest dangers: Some steady achievers may work too fast, so focused on achieving a deadline early that quality may suffer.

Build on your strengths: If you have someone on your team who is a steady achiever, you may be mismatching their capacity to perform. Their workload could be too small, and you could be stretching their capability further.

When you reflect where you fall on the thoughtfully ruthless deadline tracker, the greatest question to answer is this: What is your thinking time and action time relative to the task? For my first article, perhaps 37 hours was acceptable, but after that I needed to speed up. Are you paying attention to where your team could be burning excessive energy and time on tasks that don't merit it or perhaps achieving a deadline too early without giving it the proper thought and attention?

Finally, consider what your natural style is and don't try and replicate someone else. Ask your team what their preferred method of achieving deadlines is. Then look at your whole team profile and consider how can you build on the strengths of the individuals on your team.

If you follow these guidelines for creating your own silence and space, you will free yourself up to focus more on the long term and give yourself valuable thinking time to explore the possibilities of growth for your business for you and your organization.

Part III

THOUGHTFULLY RUTHLESS WITH YOUR ENERGY

Many popular productivity books focus on managing your time, but the crucial part of freeing up your time is also identifying how you build, sustain, and turbo boost your energy, continuously. You can complete a more in-depth assessment for free by visiting www.valwrightconsulting.com/thoughtfullyruthless. Go online to www .valwrightconsulting.com/thoughtfullyruthless and take a look at your answers to questions 11–20 in your *thoughtfully ruthless executive assessment* as you read the next two chapters to identify where you have opportunities to be even more thoughtfully ruthless with how you manage your energy.

Chapter 7

BECOMING IMPERTURBABLE

The greatest test of how you manage your energy is to think about an important upcoming event and consider where you spend your energy before, during, and after it. Perhaps it is a meeting with your board, a crucial presentation to your executive team, or speaking at a conference. Whatever it is, thoughtfully ruthless leaders know how to manage the worry trifecta to their advantage. The three stages can either leave you feeling like you are sinking in quicksand or give you the solid, steady ground you need.

HOW TO STOP THE WORRY TRIFECTA

Pre-worry

While preparation is wise, a complete virtual run-through of a conversation or important meeting is expending unnecessary energy. It is helpful to consider the possible outcomes and visualize questions and obstacles and how you may improve your probability of success, but excessive pre-worry is a waste of time and your energy.

One of the clients who I mentor has a very successful consulting practice, and she was asking my advice about a potential client. She was worried about the legal documents that the potential client may want her to sign. She asked my advice on how to negotiate elements of the contract that included payment terms, nondisclosure agreements, and working arrangements. She worried a lot about how she would request changes and how she would manage their reactions, and she wanted to talk about it. Although it was not settled that her potential client was going to actually become a client, my mentee wanted to be prepared.

This paranoid preparedness is excessive, and I refused to offer advice until she had an agreement with her client, but still she worried, despite my telling her to "just stop it!" Even the procurement team got involved with wanting to talk about the detailed requirements of the contract that had not yet been agreed to. Much to her disappointment, she never did reach agreement with her potential new client, so all of that worry, conversation, and mental energy was completely futile, but it could have taken up even more energy and time. The one lesson she did learn and is acting on is not to expend energy on items until the appropriate time. Getting the right balance of preparing purposefully will help release unnecessary wasted energy.

Parallel Worry

We've all seen comics with the thought bubbles that appear next to the character's head. Well, from time to time we all have distracting thought bubbles pop up. When we're engaging in parallel worry, those thought bubbles pop up too much and you pay more attention to them than to what is happening right in front of you. This leads to distraction. While daydreaming during a tedious meeting may be a welcome distraction from the mundane, parallel worry is a much more troubling affliction. If you parallel worry, you start to pay more attention to the voice in your head than to the voices in front of you.

Parallel worry could be about anything. You may be wondering when to make your point, you may be wondering why someone is looking at you in a puzzled fashion, you may be thinking that you didn't say the right thing 30 seconds ago. Regardless of the subject of your parallel worry, you are not listening to what you should be listening to. Think about what it's like to be working on your laptop in a coffee shop when the people seated next to you are having an animated conversation. Similarly, when you parallel worry, it is impossible to commit your full attention to a person or to your work when you are having a conversation with yourself in your head! The only way to press the virtual mute button on yourself is to notice what you are doing and bring yourself back into the reality of the moment. Afterwards you can ask yourself why you're having that conversation in your head rather than the one you need to be having. By identifying why it is hard to stay in the moment and addressing that, you will help yourself become a better listener and save precious energy.

Post-Worry

Are you prone to replaying whole events in your mind? Perhaps with subtitles of what you wish you had said, what you forgot to mention, or what you wish you had said differently?

It is too easy to play regret-roulette over things you cannot control and let your mind spin you dizzy. Frequently my coaching clients call me when a meeting hasn't gone as they expected and agonize over it by rehashing it with me (after they've replayed it in their minds several times). I tell them they have to follow three quick steps to eliminate post-worry: Reflect, learn, and act. First you have to reflect on whether you achieved what you set out to achieve. Often I hear complaints over minor issues that are inconsequential. Worrying that you got into a heated debate or that half of your audience asked you tough questions may not matter if you achieved what you set out to. Once you have reflected on what happened, you have to decide what you can learn from it. Could you have prepared better? Could you have been in the moment and listened more? Did you react too emotionally? Decide what you can learn. The final step is the most forgotten one: action. It is easy to inwardly learn and reflect, but to take action in public or private requires an openness and willingness to be vulnerable and experiment with different ways of working. Sometimes the best action can be to forget about it!

As the *worry transformer diagram* in Figure 7.1 illustrates, this will help you turn your pre-worry into purposeful planning, your parallel worry to being able to listen and be in the moment, and your post-worry into thoughtfully reviewing success and taking action. Use the *worry trifecta assessment* to identify which areas of your whole life cause you to lose the most energy. Rate yourself if you are an obsessive worrier, a distracted worrier, or thoughtfully ruthless with how you manage your thoughts and worries.

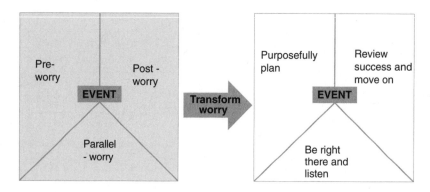

Figure 7.1   Transforming the Worry Trifecta

WORRY TRIFECTA EXERCISE

Rate yourself against the eight situations below and you can also add your own. For each situation, determine how much worry you do before, during, and after a situation. Evaluate your level of worry like this:

- Obsessive—Worrying dominates your thoughts and it can consume you.
- Distracted worrier—Like an annoying buzzing fridge in the corner of the room, worrying is a distraction that often grabs your attention and causes you to sporadically loose focus.
- Thoughtfully ruthless—You intentionally focus your energy to prepare without being paralyzed and pre-think without becoming obsessed.

	Pre-Worry	Parallel Worry	Post-Worry
Meeting with your board or executive leadership team			
An interview for a job you really want			
Speaking at a conference or company meeting			

	Pre-Worry	Parallel Worry	Post-Worry
Giving difficult feedback to a peer or someone on your team			
Pitching an idea for a new product or service			
Declining invitations to social events			
Shamelessly talking about your achievements			
Asking for and receiving feedback			
Insert your own here			
Insert your own here			

RAPID THOUGHT TO ACTION

It starts with taking control of where and how you expend your energy when you are in specific situations, but the benefits multiply from there. A key differentiation of a thoughtfully ruthless leader is how quickly he or she can move from an idea to concrete action. I have seen this work and fail most dramatically when considering acquisition targets. I have observed many conversations where talk and ideas about acquisitions float around almost like a discussion about possible restaurant choices for dinner. Everyone has an opinion, no one is willing to make a decision, and everyone is clueless how a decision will be made. As a result, energy and precious time are wasted.

There is a better way! Follow these six steps to accelerate your thoughts to action:

1. **Say it out loud to yourself.** Then give yourself a couple of days to see if it still resonates as important to you.
2. **Test it with your inner circle of advisors.** Sound out those who you trust and have your best interests at heart to get advice.
3. **Develop a rapid plan to consider the idea.** This is where most people and ideas stall: the idea stays as just an idea without becoming a plan that could expose holes or new opportunities in your original idea.

4. **Create criteria for success.** Decide how you will decide whether to move forward.
5. **Operate a fast-go/no-go system.** Just like product development cycles need clear gates and go/no-go decision points, so do new ideas. Set a clear time limit.
6. **Once decided, don't wallow or revisit unless there is a meaningful change.**

I have sat through countless go/no-go for video games, new devices, and unique services. Deep in an organization companies often employ the rigor of these six steps, but I rarely see such rigor at the executive leadership level where ideas are bounced around but not always grabbed and considered thoughtfully and systematically. And I rarely see this helpful technique employed in people's lives outside of business. Decisions about whether to move house, buy a new car, emigrate, or take a month-long summer holiday float around and absorb excessive energy with no forward progress. Consider a decision you have been wrestling with, and follow these steps to get to action and a decision today.

HOW IMPERTURBABLE ARE YOU?

How do you react to the unexpected? Think of it: the decision you fully expected the board to approve just got blocked, your top employee just quit, or you can't get Wi-Fi access when you desperately need it. Whatever the unexpected disappointment is, the way you react and what you show on the outside affects your own energy and the energy of those around you. The speed with which you can brush it off and refocus will determine how fast you achieve what you set out to do. The key is having a strong protective barrier.

As the *imperturbable barrier diagram* in Figure 7.2 shows, many things can knock you off course and disrupt whether you achieve what you set out to and in the process these things will absorb your time, mess up your priorities, and sap your energy. To counteract this potential disruption, you need to create a barrier that acts like solar panels on a roof: it collects the excess energy and deflects the heat so that you stay cool and in control.

It sounds so simple, yet it is easy to get wrapped up in the moment and lose your cool. I used to work with a leader who was obsessed with reading online reviews and community forums. In the games industry this can be a

Are You Imperturbable?

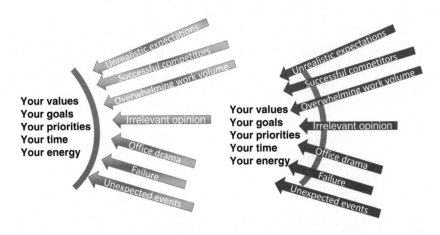

What breaks your barrier?

Figure 7.2 The Imperturbable Barrier Diagram

full-time job in and of itself, but he liked to stay connected with the customers who used to play our products, so he would read them continuously. If he just read them and moved on with his day, it would have been fine. But if there was a negative comment about a new game, or a demo that had been released, or about an interview he had done, it would knock him off course for hours, sometimes days. He didn't know how to observe, listen, and decide whether he was going to act or ignore the feedback, so he would wallow in it and get riled up, even when it came from a gamer-forum that wasn't known for the most positive discussions of the games industry. He needed to learn to be more imperturbable.

Often just writing down how you are feeling can be enough to process your emotions and move on. Try using a journal, or making a note in Evernote or your own virtual notebook. Pay attention to how you are feeling and why. Be specific and describe the event, what the trigger was, and how you were feeling. Also, try fast forwarding and ask yourself: Will this be important to me in three months? In twelve? Doing so may give you the perspective you need. Laughter also works. I remember working with Peter Moore when he was leading Xbox. *South Park* featured him in an episode, and rather than getting riled up, Peter found it hilarious and shared the links and pictures all over his Twitter and Facebook feeds. He even has a sculpture of his character behind his desk as COO of Electronic Arts.

Laughing at yourself or a situation is sometimes the best way to respond, but you also need to be clear on your overall purpose and focus. Put up a visual reminder of your goals for the year, the month, and the day. If you feel yourself getting sidetracked, ask yourself if it will help progress your goals; if not, quickly focus your energy on what will accelerate your results. If all else fails, having a strong inner circle of advisors will help support you when you need it, and having someone you can call to vent or get advice will help keep your focus.

Remember that your energy and emotion are contagious—they rub off on your team and everyone else you interact with. Just like the movie *Inside Out* depicts, it is easy for another emotion to take over and control you. Take notice of whether anger, disgust, or fear are battling for control of you and your virtual headquarters. Your team and peers are watching, absorbing, and trying to maintain their own protective barrier to being imperturbable too!

MANAGING THE ENERGY LEAKS

As California experiences the worst drought on record, leaky pipes cause up to 16 percent of California's water to be lost. The same waste occurs in companies on a much larger scale. Wasted energy can severely hamper a business's ability to hit product deadlines or sales targets.

Take a look at the *energy equilibrium diagram* in Figure 7.3 and rate where your team spends its energy.

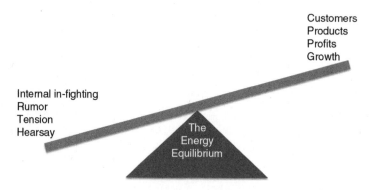

Figure 7.3 Energy Equilibrium Diagram

When you walk around your offices, overhearing conversations in hallways and at lunch, what are people talking about? Are they discussing your customers, your products, the latest industry news, how to accelerate innovation, or how to improve your profit? Or are they talking about why marketing didn't do what they should have, or the real reason they have heard about why that acquisition stalled, or that they don't understand why the latest vice president promotion was *that* leader? The greatest outpouring of wasted energy in companies is the wasted energy on internal drama—the unnecessary speculation, pontification, and gossip.

Common Triggers for Going Off Balance

Knowing the common causes of energy leaks can prepare you to better manage them. Here is a list of common triggers that can cause people to lose their balance. Consider how both you and your team may react to these various situations and how you recover and help your team to do so too.

- When there is a change in strategy
- When a product is woefully unsuccessful
- When a competitor launches a remarkable product or service
- When a new leader is hired
- When a PR disaster occurs
- When the stock rapidly drops
- When there is a significant change in the industry
- When someone leaves unexpectedly
- Close to bonus payout time
- When a promotion occurs
- For an undisclosed personal reason

Addressing Energy Leaks

Now you know the triggers; simply noticing and getting curious will help you and your team stem the leaks of energy. There are five ways to address energy leaks:

1. Be more transparent than secretive.
2. Be as honest as possible.
3. Be thoughtful about who you communicate what to—full disclosure and honesty may not always work everywhere.

4. Overcommunicate repeatedly.
5. Stop to listen and adjust.

YOUR ACCELERATORS AND DECELERATORS

Knowing your own personal accelerators and decelerators will help you manage your energy.

Think back to a time when you were at your most productive. What was unique about that situation, your role, the people, or your location? You want to identify where you are at your most productive and then replicate it.

Using either a journal or a virtual notebook, list all the factors that accelerate your energy and performance. Think about the time of day, the music you listen to (or the silence you need), the location, how much sleep you have had, who you are spending your time with, the type of work you are doing, the type of boss you have, the company you are working for, the meaning and purpose of your work, and how you are contributing to your community. All of these factors may feature in your accelerators.

Now consider all of the factors that decelerate your performance and list those. When are you at your least productive? What situations cause you the most frustration? What exhausts you and drives you to the point of distraction so that you cannot concentrate? These things may be the obvious opposite of your accelerators, but list them anyway.

You become more thoughtfully ruthless with your energy by repeatedly creating situations that contain your accelerators and avoiding situations that are your decelerators.

When I complete this exercise with executives, there are three common factors that consistently show up: what you eat, how much sleep you get, and whether you are taking part in your favorite exercise at the right frequency for you, so we will dive into those three accelerators and decelerators in a lot more detail.

ACCELERATING BY IMPROVING YOUR SLEEP, NUTRITION, AND EXERCISE

If I told you that you could improve your own and your team's productivity by 20 percent, you would likely want me to tell you how right now. That's what I'll do, but here is my disclaimer: I am not a doctor, a nutritionist, or a fitness expert (despite having my CrossFit Level 1 certification, so technically I could run a CrossFit class but I never will, as I know my limits). My guidance here is pragmatic and observational. It comes from a quarter of a century observing leaders when they are at their peak of performance and when they are making disastrous mistakes. There is one common thread that you do not have to be a doctor to figure out: those who get the right sleep, nutrition, and exercise feel more energetic, make decisions faster, have more fun, are more focused, and spend more time imagining the possibilities rather than fearing the worst.

Proper sleep, nutrition, and exercise provide the fastest productivity gain you can make—and it is within your control. Many make the mistake of thinking healthy choices are a personal decision, but I believe we should all look at it as a business decision. People seek out books on nutrition or hire a personal trainer when they are looking to get fit. It is not their first action when they want to improve their productivity, but it should be.

Despite the multibillion-dollar combined industries of fitness, nutrition, and sleep experts, people are exhausted and unfit. Most people know what to do but they don't do it for one simple reason: they don't connect the downside with the upside in productivity. It's simple: Sleep, balanced nutrition, and regular exercise will improve your business performance, but no one says so.

Sleep

Studies have shown that driving while sleep deprived makes you as impaired as driving while under the influence of alcohol, yet few people treat sleep as important. British Prime Minister Margaret Thatcher was an anomaly; just because she could run Britain on four hours of sleep a night does not mean you should try to run your team or company on that.

If you are still reading this chapter and haven't skipped to the next one, chances are you aren't getting the sleep, nutrition, and exercise that you need, or you are conscious enough to want to explore what the potential upside is of being rested, energized, and at your peak level of performance.

Michael Affronti, VP of Product Development for Thinking Phones, gets up at 4:22 AM every day. Here is how he describes his routine:

4:22 AM – Alarm goes off
I set it for 4:22 AM because I believe that waking on the quarter or half hour makes it easy to say, "I'll just sleep for another 15 (or 30)

minutes." Sleeping an extra eight minutes feels less useful to me and gives me the incentive to get up.

4:30 AM – Chore duties

I feed the cats and do house chores.

4:40 AM – Learn

I'm trying to relearn Italian this year, so I spend 10 minutes every morning using Duolingo to practice different lessons.

4:50 AM – Read

I spend about 15 minutes reading tech news sites. Long articles get sent to Pocket for reading on the train.

5:05 AM – House logistics

I use this time to update our budget and deal with any household logistics.

5:15 AM – Plan my day

I spend the last 10 minutes of this part of the morning reviewing my calendar for the day.

5:25 AM – Get to the gym

Get ready for the gym and bike to CrossFit. I usually get there about 15 minutes early to stretch and warm up.

6:00 AM – Workout/blog

I work out at CrossFit South Brooklyn on Mondays, Wednesdays, and Thursdays during the week, and both Saturday and Sunday on the weekend. Tuesdays and Fridays are rest days in our gym's CrossFit programming, and on those days I use this hour to work on my blog.

7:15 AM – Cook, eat, triage

After I bike home from the gym, I cook a quick breakfast. While I eat breakfast I take my first look at my work e-mail, reviewing urgent threads, and seeing what came in overnight.

8:30 AM – Head to work

Leave for work. I *love* the R train.

If just reading this exhausts you, that's okay, you are not alone. But it works for Michael, and for more than 15 years he has experimented and found what gives him peak productivity. The critical part is finding what works for you, not pretending to be Michael or Margaret Thatcher.

Parents know how precious sleep is. Those first few weeks with a newborn test your ability to perform on minimal and infrequent sleep.

I remember quite clearly how that first time you get a block of four continuous hours sleep after weeks of 90-minute blocks, you feel refreshed, revived, and energized. Your body quickly adapts to how much sleep you are giving it and survives—but surviving is not thriving.

Walk along the sidewalk a block away from the entrance to a corporate office block or campus near you and just stop and watch. Pay attention to the body language, facial expressions, and level of energy in everyone's walk. What can you determine from five minutes of observation? I often do this at my client buildings—just wait in the morning and watch. Are people buzzing with excitement and conversation or are people slowly trudging into the office?

Living in Southern California, I get to walk my daughters to school most days of the week throughout the whole year. If you have ever watched five- and seven-year-olds walk to school, that is where you see excitement and energy. They have so much energy in the morning that they skip, hop, and cartwheel the mile walk to school. I tell them to run to the third tree and do 20 jumping jacks while I catch up. Imagine if you could capture the energy and excitement of a five year old? Well you can with the *sleep revival plan*.

Sleep Revival Plan

First take some time for reflection. Ask yourself the following three questions and write your answers in a journal or virtual notebook:

1. What is your wake up routine?
2. What is your pre-sleep routine?
3. Do you take naps? Like clockwork or spontaneously?

Now ask yourself have you ever felt these Sleep Insanity Signs? (Trust me, SIS is much worse than SOS.)

- Do you ever feel like you might fall asleep at the wheel when driving?
- Do you fall asleep watching TV or a movie?
- Do you ever crave a nap in the middle of the day when you are at work?
- Do you snooze your alarm more than once in the morning?
- Do you have difficulty falling asleep?
- Do you wake in the middle of the night and find yourself unable to quickly return to sleep?

- Do you fall asleep before your kids when you are reading them a bedtime story?
- Do you consistently refuse social invitations because you are simply too tired and would rather sleep than socialize?

Popular wisdom says you need eight hours sleep a night, but at around 9 PM in the evening logic and reasoning fight with your desire to watch a movie, continue with household chores, talk to friends, or go out and socialize. The most crucial part is that you have to find the right rhythm for you. If you want to experiment with your sleep try the 1 × 7 test. Add one hour of sleep a night to your usual sleep time, continue for the full seven days, and then afterward reflect on how you feel at the end of the seven days.

Another method to improve your sleep is to write a sleep diary. Make note of the time you go to bed, how long you sleep, if you wake in the night and how easily you went back to sleep, and what time you wake in the morning. Also note what your pre-sleep routine was and whether your food and drink intake was different than usual. After a couple of weeks you will have enough information to analyze and see what patterns emerge.

There is another solution that is as simple as breathing in and breathing out. Dr. Andrew Weil, a Harvard-trained medical doctor, has researched a simple breathing technique that helps you fall asleep, stay asleep, and get back to sleep if you wake in the middle of the night. Everyone I have recommended it to in my statistically insignificant testing over a period of a few months has reported significant success with it.

The 4–7–8 (or Relaxing Breath) exercise is almost too simple to be believable. Place the tip of your tongue against the ridge of tissue just behind your upper front teeth, and keep it there through the entire exercise. You will be exhaling through your mouth around your tongue; try pursing your lips slightly if this seems awkward.

- Exhale completely through your mouth, making a whoosh sound.
- Close your mouth and inhale quietly through your nose to a mental count of four.
- Hold your breath for a count of seven.
- Exhale completely through your mouth, making a whoosh sound to a count of eight.
- This is one breath. Now inhale again and repeat the cycle three more times for a total of four breaths.

Dr. Weil states that this is a natural tranquilizer for the nervous system. Unlike tranquilizing drugs, which are often effective when you first take them but then lose their power over time, this exercise is subtle when you first try it but gains in power with repetition and practice. Do it at least twice a day. You cannot do it too frequently. Do not do more than four breaths at one time for the first month of practice. Later, if you wish, you can extend it to eight breaths. If you feel a little lightheaded when you first breathe this way, do not be concerned; it will pass.

Once you develop this technique by practicing it every day, it will be a very useful tool that you will always have with you. Use it whenever anything upsetting happens—before you react. Use it whenever you are aware of internal tension. Use it to help yourself fall asleep. This exercise cannot be recommended too highly. Everyone can benefit from it.

The next area that will improve your sleep and increase your energy is going old school with your devices. When everyone else is buying one of the 45 million wearables that will be sold by the end of this year, you may want to run in the opposite direction to drastically increase your energy. The true secret to improved productivity involves stepping back in time and detaching yourself from your smartphone, smartwatch, and any other device that beeps, buzzes, or tempts you into the distraction zone. Many of my clients experiment with this over a 30-day period.

First, dust off your wristwatch. I have an exquisite Tag Heuer watch that I bought 11 years ago in Dubai on the way to our honeymoon in the Maldives. I had stopped wearing it because I always have my phone so close by and that's what most of us use these days to tell time. Except, of course, I rarely used my phone just to check the time; I might also look at a news site, my e-mail, or Twitter, leading to distraction. It was a delight to start wearing my watch again—though it took some time before I remembered to actually look at it! Now that I am relying on my watch again, I've found that my phone stays in my purse or pocket a lot longer, and I am more focused.

Second, start using a traditional alarm clock. Alarm clock sales are at an all-time low because many people now use the alarm on their phone for their morning wake-up call. Duracell has suffered a 4 percent drop in sales that they attribute in part to a decline in digital radio alarms, and Procter & Gamble has plans to spin off that business. Keeping your phone by your bed creates a lot of consequences for you personally: It can lead to many distractions just at the point when you need to relax, and it can actually prevent you from falling asleep. Once you wake, the phone at your bedside means you probably start your day by looking at e-mail, tweets, Facebook posts, and other messages. Could you leave your phone in another room or at least across the other side of your bedroom? Try putting your favorite book on your nightstand for a more gentle end to your day so you can wake up refreshed and focused.

The final way that you can keep your phone in your pocket or purse is to start carrying around your camera again. I dusted off my camera from the back of the cupboard, and I have been enjoying taking endless photos without getting distracted by other things. A study by the University of Washington of caregivers at playgrounds revealed that 44 percent of caregivers felt that they should minimize the use of cell phones while watching children play; yet, they felt guilty that they failed to live up to that standard. Using a camera rather than a cell phone for taking pictures could help with that! Even when out at a restaurant, it is far more acceptable to have your camera out to take pictures than to use your phone. When you use your phone, your companions may think you are also checking e-mail or Facebook at the same time!

Nutrition

This is going to be the shortest piece of advice you will ever read on nutrition: *Find out what works for you and stick to it.* The end.

Okay, a little explanation: I have found talking about nutrition to be more controversial than religion, so I am not giving any advice on it other than my one nutrition rule above. Whether you are vegan, paleo, carb-loading, carb-loving, carb-hating, plant-loving, juicing, or addicted to protein shakes, I really do not care. What I do care about is that you are paying attention to your nutrition and you have a plan and stick to it.

Microsoft used to offer an incredible free benefit to its employees: Free nutrition coaching and guidance with their free local gym. You would see employees transformed over a period of several months as they changed what they ate. The plan was irrelevant; the priceless part was the account-ability. The program that had a $4,000 value was free if you hit your target goals. That level of commitment meant nobody signed up unless they genuinely believed they could stick with it and hit their goals. If you need to change what you eat, consider how you can be held accountable to change and stick with it.

Exercise

Thoughtfully ruthless leaders are selfish about the exercise they need to maintain their energy and focus. Those who run a marathon need weeks and months of training to condition their body throughout the year and perform on race day. I see this with peaks and troughs in product development cycles. There are always crunch times, unexpected delays, and last minute herculean pushes, but you need to be at peak performance so you can tap into your energy reserves for those rare situations.

If you watch any athlete, how they perform in the final minutes or seconds shows how much stamina and strength they have. One of my CrossFit coaches, Paul Lee, was performing in the CrossFit Games Open qualifiers. Watching how he performed in the final 15 seconds was inspiring. He didn't slow down; in fact, he sped up. He increased his focus and managed three extra snatch lifts of 75lb in the last 10 seconds. That is the sign of an elite athlete. How you perform as a deadline approaches separates the elite from the successful leaders.

Ranan Lachman, CEO of the toy-sharing company, Pley, is an Ironman athlete; he attributes his focus and success to his Ironman training and finds his inspiration there: "There is a point in most races where you want to quit, where no one will know or care if you quit apart from you, so you dig deep and find the energy and motivation to keep going."

Just as the toughest part of the Ironman calls for tenacity and determination, so does managing the cash flow and investment choices as he builds a multibillion-dollar business. You need to make exhaustion the exception, not the rule. Just like you wouldn't run a marathon like a series of 200m sprints, you have to pace yourself.

As we discussed in your selfish charter in Chapter 3, thoughtfully ruthless leaders prioritize their own exercise schedule. Sari Davison, CEO of BooginHead, built her multimillion-dollar business while always prioritizing her own time at the gym. "I am selfish, I always take time for myself. I am not effective in my job without my time away, at the gym or yoga. I need to take time away and I do that ruthlessly."

All of these aspects will increase your energy from the inside out. The next crucial piece is how you increase your energy from the outside in by who you surround yourself with and how rapidly you draw the right people in and repel those you need to away.

Chapter 8

DIVORCE YOUR FRIENDS AND NETWORK

Twelve of us started the Management Training Scheme at the same time, at the British department store retailer House of Fraser. The prestige of being associated with parent company Harrods was exhilarating. We were assigned our first departments, and I was given the radio and TV department where I would learn everything there was to know about TVs, music systems, and the then ever-so-popular digital compact cassette (DCC) by Phillips. Over our 12-month program, we all progressed at a similar pace, each with the ultimate goal of becoming an assistant department manager within the store. One of the team got promoted first, and I was delighted. She had much more experience and guts than the rest of us, but the dynamic of the friendly group changed towards her. It felt like high school again; she was not included in social events and jealously driven comments distracted many times we were together as a group. That was my first ever experience of workplace drama and, unfortunately, not my last. After my first promotion to assistant training manager, training the 1,000-strong store team on customer service, sales skills, and management skills, I was offered an opportunity to cover a maternity leave at the Cheltenham store in our region. I realized I had to make friends fast and build peer relationships faster if I was to influence and have success in a store where I knew nobody, and I had to learn how fast.

It is easy to hold onto old friends and previous peers by habit. They may not be negative people (though some are), but those who are living life at a different speed than you may be secretly holding you back. This chapter explains what creates an enviable inner circle. Once you assess where you are, it gives you a fast how-to guide to upgrade it if you don't have the inner circle you need. Thoughtfully ruthless leaders associate themselves with other thoughtfully ruthless leaders; to do this, you need to know how to seek them out, to agree how to stay connected, and to build mutually beneficial relationships with your peers. Learn how to spot a pacemaker in your peer group and learn to race alongside them. Finally, the chapter explores how to assess whether you have believers or doubters around you and how to surround yourself with people who have confidence and faith in you. Too often people are not ruthless enough to ditch those who blatantly or inadvertently doubt, criticize, or fail to delight in your success. While some ruthlessness is commonly accepted in your business circles, it is in your personal circles where you need to be the most ruthless.

When you are on a rapid success trajectory, quickly evaluate who you spend your precious social time with. While you don't want to abandon every previous friend you have ever had, you do want to ask yourself whether your friends are truly your friends.

Use these *five friendship warning signs* to conduct a quick friendship evaluation test:

1. They tell others, not you directly, why they are not happy with you.
2. They make passive-aggressive comments: "Wow, you get to travel so much for your job. That must be fun for you but so hard for your children."
3. They don't celebrate your successes with you. As Andrea Leigh, general manager of Amazon Canada says, "A friend who holds you back was never really your friend to begin with. If they are not supporting maximizing your success, they don't care about you."
4. You dread, rather than look forward to spending time with them.
5. After spending time with them, you are exhausted or miserable, rather than energized and inspired.

THE GREENHOUSE EFFECT

If you unnecessarily hold onto old friends and colleagues, you will suppress your success like tomatoes in a greenhouse deprived of sunlight. You may not wilt and fail to produce fruit, but if you had more sunshine in your life by way of inspirational positive friends, then your growth and fruit yield would be much more prolific. Much networking advice talks about your colleagues and your peers inside and outside of your company and industry, but that misses the most vital part—your friends. This is one of the toughest areas to be ruthless in your life, particularly as you may have much shared history, successes, and great memories, but you need to consider in a thoughtful way who is it time to move on from so you have free time to spend making new connections and relationships.

The rules for evaluating friendships also apply to all relationships at work, in our community, and daily life. To know how much you are suppressing your results, we first have to consider the three critical factors to successful business and personal relationships (see Figure 8.1):

1. Access
2. Value
3. Frequency

First, you need to know who you need to know. Perfecting your connections starts with making those relationships to begin with. Second, you need to provide mutual value to each other. You both must feel the benefit of spending time together, whether you are learning from each

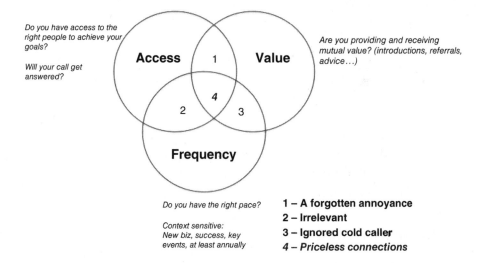

Figure 8.1 Perfecting Your Connections

other, helping each other's business, or just having fun together. Finally, just like Goldilocks likes her porridge just right, you can't be too hot on the heels of always wanting to spend time with someone, and you cannot go cold on them and forget about them for months on end. To get into the sweet spot of the perfect connection, you have to get the balance perfectly right, which may require some adaptations along the way.

This is what it looks like when it is not quite perfect:

- If you have access to people and offer value but get the frequency wrong by either overwhelming them with invites or forgetting them, you will become a forgotten annoyance.
- If you have the access and time just right but haven't established that there is mutual value, you will be irrelevant to each other.
- If you get the frequency right and have mutual value to offer each other but don't have a qualified introduction, then you will be ignored like the cold-caller that you are.

Here are some action steps to improve each area:

- Frequency: Ask and agree how often you will stay connected; revisit this to make sure it is working for both of you.
- Access: Only ask for and provide qualified introductions. Don't spam people's in-box with "you have to meet" requests. Ask both parties before introducing someone if they want to be connected and ask others to do the same for you.
- Value: This is where you need to be thoughtful about where you can expect mutually beneficial value. Consider what you can provide and what you would like to gain in return.

Robert Cialdini, author of *Influence: The Psychology of Persuasion*, names six principles of influence; one of them is reciprocity, which is particularly important when building your connections. Offering something of value first before making a request has been proven to increase the likelihood that someone will say yes to your follow-up request.

There are three common failings I see with executive networks. Don't fall into these traps:

1. *Forgetting to consciously assess social and professional* relationships to ensure they are providing mutual value and benefits.

2. *Failing to press refresh on professional and social circles* when you are promoted, take a new role, or make a gargantuan leap in your career. Old friendships and work relationships can drain your energy and your time if they are past their usefulness date. Living in aspirational circles will catapult your impact and learning.
3. *Forgetting to ask for help.* It is easy to forget to ask for introductions. Pay attention and dedicate some regular time every few months to do a bit of research and intentionally attend to your connections.

Your social circle is of the utmost importance, and it is the least attended to by leaders everywhere. When I was talking to a remarkably successful executive recently and I shared him my "divorce your friends" concept, he said to me, "Val, you are spot on. Will you please tell my wife? Every weekend she drags me to dinner parties and fundraisers that I do not want to attend, where I have no fun and no desire to talk to anyone. Yet there are all of these other couples that I would love to spend time with, but we don't have an empty slot in our social calendar for months!"

This is where your thoughtfully ruthless social circle has to be a joint effort with your significant other. It's important to jointly agree how, who, and where you spend your discretionary time.

PUT YOUR SOCIAL LIFE ON AUTOPILOT

One of the greatest challenges of a successful executive's social life is the logistics and prioritization. Have you ever realized that it has been months since you saw your favorite friends? When our twins arrived and our oldest daughter wasn't quite two years old, my husband and I knew we needed to take ruthless action to save our sanity. Parents of multiples find it is easy to lose touch with their friends just when they need them the most. Ongoing work deadlines can have the same effect.

My twins have taught me to put my social life on autopilot. I did this with a close group of friends in Seattle. We decided to meet the first Monday of every month; whoever could make it that night would show up. We picked the venue for the following month at the end of each dinner. It required zero planning or follow-up e-mails. Don't rely on yourself to remember to make plans. People are busy. Consider how can you autopilot your social life.

I hear phrases like this from busy executives all the time: "I owe my partner." "I need to pay him [or her] back for the last six months of my crazy work schedule." "My partner isn't happy with how much time I spend at work."

It's okay to need some alone time with your partner. It's okay for your partner to need that from you. There. I have said it. I love my kids, and I also love my husband. Sometimes our conversations revolve solely around tasks, schedules, chores, and parenting. That can be no fun. We have always prioritized date nights once a month and date weekends twice a year. My three daughters have taught me that I have to be intentional. It is easy to allow family and business commitments to take over everything. Rather than sitting back and letting that happen, consider how you can schedule your social and personal time as efficiently as you schedule your work commitments.

Your social circle is one of five components of your perfect network. Now that you know how to assess your connections, review the network analysis in Figure 8.2 and score yourself against the five components of the Perfect Connections.

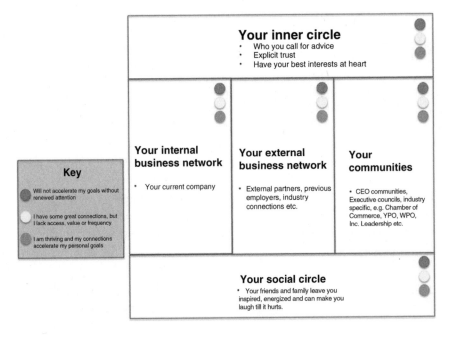

Figure 8.2 Your Network Analysis

Assess each of the areas: Your inner circle, your internal business network, your external business network, your communities, and your social circle and rate them red, yellow, or green, depending on how much they are helping you accelerate your goals.

Now pick one priority area that you will focus on first. Decide what one action you can take to improve those connections and then make the call or ask for advice on that area before coming back and systematically working through each of the areas.

AN ENVIABLE INNER CIRCLE OF ADVISORS

Imagine you have an incredible opportunity to sell your company, take a promotion, make a significant acquisition, or perhaps hire someone who could be your successor. Who would you call for advice? It is hoped two or three names immediately popped into your head. Now ask yourself, would they immediately take or return your call? Would they be willing to provide you candid feedback, acting with your best interests at heart? Have you stayed in touch with them recently so they know all the context about your business and your life?

The number of those questions you answered with a wholehearted yes reveals how strong your inner circle is. It is not unusual for a CEO or executive to be so absorbed in his company, his team, building products, and servicing customers that he lets his inner circle fall down the list of priorities. If yours needs a little attention, schedule time into your calendar today to reinvigorate your relationships so when that opportunity presents itself and you need advice, your call will be quickly returned.

Successful marathon runners use a pacemaker to guide them to match their pace to their target so they can beat their personal best time. Thoughtfully ruthless leaders know they need pacemakers in their connections so they don't slow down at the most opportune times.

When you're identifying who you need in your connections consider these three factors:

1. Speed. You want to be connected to people who are capable of running just as fast as you, preferably slightly faster; this is where constant upgrades are necessary.
2. Uncomfortably candid. You don't need someone around who is always telling you how brilliant you are. While you want to celebrate

your successes, you also want to see the possibilities. Andrea Leigh, GM of Canada for Amazon, says, "I always seek out truth-tellers for my inner circle. At Amazon I selected two leaders who were in the painful-but-so-helpful category of leaders. The feedback was brutal at times, but one member of my inner circle was so sharp and insightful I knew I would get the truth and helpful guidance."

3. A mix of leaders. Target different leaders for different levels of support. Leigh says, "I also wanted guidance on how to stay true to my long-term goals and who I was. That was particularly helpful if I was experiencing new challenges or difficult situations when we were going through periods of high growth. I built my inner circle with different leaders who could help me in different ways." You can also get surprising advice from people who do not know your industry and company well. Leigh notes, "In my book club, I have a seventh grade teacher. She often gives me some of the best advice of all of my friends. She is not in the industry, nothing about her world is the same as mine, which is just why her advice is so valuable."

INTERNAL AND EXTERNAL CONNECTIONS

Your company culture will determine how easy it is to make and maintain internal connections. Some companies have incredible community-building events and match leaders across functions and geographies while others work completely autonomously. Some companies will actively encourage you to make industry and external connections, and others will direct your attention to your current team, project, and customers. Either way, you cannot ignore your internal and external networks because otherwise when you need them most, they won't be there for you because you have forgotten to cultivate the relationships.

COMMUNITIES

Consider which communities you want to be involved in. They could be industry or functionally focused. Alan Weiss, the rock star of consulting and author of 60 books on consulting, has the ultimate proof that community drives remarkable value. He offers free *million dollar consulting mentor summits* for anyone who is in his community, and he offers a free online forum where not only can consultants, speakers, and coaches access advice from each other, but he shows up there daily to answer questions and give advice—all completely free. The Young Presidents Organization, Entrepreneurs' Organization, and many industry-specific communities exist, usually around key industry events like CES and E3. If you don't know which community events would be best for you to attend, ask your inner circle of advisors for where they hang out and where you could get involved to broaden your connections.

PERFECTING YOUR TEAM'S CONNECTIONS

Your role as a thoughtfully ruthless leader is to help assess and improve the connections of your team. When I relocated from England to Seattle with Xbox, my manager did a fantastic job setting up my transition so I could arrive in the country and be well connected. Mary McMahon, now chief of staff on HoloLens, spent one weekend driving me around the neighborhoods of Seattle helping me get acquainted with the city and choose a neighborhood while teaching me the idiosyncrasies of life in the United States versus the United Kingdom. Mary made my transition a delight, and because of that I have always helped companies systematize that approach. When we were hiring prolifically at Amazon for our fashion business, we matched executives with local executives when they came for their interview, so they had social connections as well as business connections to make the transition easier for them and their families. Help your team take the perfecting your connections assessment and help them build improvements that will accelerate their relationships.

SURROUNDING YOURSELF WITH BELIEVERS

Victor Meldrew is a popular TV character on the British comedy program *One Foot in the Grave*. He epitomizes the grumpy old miserable British pensioner. It isn't hard to find Victors in many companies, and while being vocally self-critical is one of Amazon's defining strengths, which is explored in Chapter 11, it is done with a positive spin: with the intent to improve and learn from your mistakes, not to take an "ain't-it-awful" approach where misery loves company and Eeyore likes to be with other Eeyores.

There is a reason Monty Python's *Life of Brian* is such a popular film. If you don't know the song "Always Look on the Bright Side of Life," I suggest you take a listen and consider making it your new theme song because positivity (along with pure grit) is a defining characteristic of successful leaders. Martin Seligman, the master of positive psychology, has studies that show if you can encourage positivity, you can improve your business results.

Pessimism and optimism are contagious either way. As a leader you dramatically affect which attitude your team will spread. So make sure your inner circle is filled with people who look on the bright side of life—not Victor Meldrew's!

Chapter 9

CREATING A LEAPFROG ORGANIZATION

R apid growth is no longer the exception. With crowd-funding allowing for new and unexpected competition in unexpected places, explosive growth is just to be expected. Companies such Uber have helped to reinvent how we travel, and Airbnb is transforming the hospitality industry. New industries appear overnight, and "the-Uber-of . . ." is the latest common description in many start-up pitches to investors. Amazon is now using its customers to deliver packages and has launched Amazon-Now, a service that guarantees customers' orders within an hour by tapping into its 244 million customers to deliver packages. While lawmakers play catch-up to update ancient laws to reflect the flexible reality of the new sharing economy, Amazon customers will get to benefit from faster delivery times and Amazon's growth will continue at warp speed.

Amazon is proving that big companies can out-share the start-ups in the sharing economy, disrupting their current business models and building on the strengths they already have. But product innovation isn't enough; a ruthless approach to your resources is needed, in a thoughtful way.

YOUR FIVE-YEAR LEAP

Given this rapid growth, too many leaders hire for their current company rather than for the size and scale it will be in five years' time. By assessing the capability and capacity of your organization against your future business, you begin to understand the gap you need to close to create your leapfrog organization and catapult to success. Since rapid growth is the new norm, you need to build your organization of the future, today. Doing so means you will likely go through the *Intentional Annoyance Phase* and displease many of your existing people to realize the growth your company is capable of — but that is necessary if you truly want to catapult innovation.

The reality is that from my observations 75 percent of hiring has the effect of slowing you down rather than speeding you up because of the catastrophic fault most hiring mangers make: They hire for their immediate needs today, not for what they need in the future. You need to be ruthless, in a thoughtful way, with your resources. You have to approach change, hiring, and growth in a completely different way. By adhering to the following steps you can create your own leapfrog organization.

Step One: Pick a Time Horizon

It starts first with knowing the size and scale of your business in two years' time — but don't get stuck on the time horizon. When I used to work at Land Rover, our strategy sessions focused on ten years out, so we would start with a five-year leap. When I worked with rapidly growing consumer electronics companies, we focused on a two-year leap. Pick a time horizon to coincide with your next significant growth leap.

Step Two: Know Your Current and Future Business

First take a look at your business today and note your profit, revenue, and employees. Consider what markets you are currently in, which industries, and what products and services you offer. Now leap ahead to your first leap. What will be different? Ask yourself these questions:

- What new markets will we be in?
- What new products will we offer?
- What new services might we develop?
- Where will our locations be based?
- How will we have grown (by acquisition, organically)?

Step Three: Live in Your Future World

Next, imagine you are living in your business in your two-year leap. Start by considering your own role and that of your CEO: How will that be different? What skills and capabilities will you need? Which of those do you have already? Now ask yourself the toughest question every CEO has to ask themselves: Is it time for me to fire myself?

If you are not the CEO, and you are a member of the board, or the executive team, this may be a more difficult conversation to have. But if you avoid it, you are suffocating the growth and innovation possibilities of your company, so you have a choice to make.

It may not be as radical as firing yourself or your CEO, but it may be time to decide that you do not have the perfect CEO for your leapfrog organization, which we explore later in this chapter. But assuming you have the right CEO now, take a look at your executive team and ask yourself these questions:

- What are the pivotal capabilities we need to support our future growth?
- Which of those do we have today in our existing executive team?
- Which can we develop and grow?
- What do we need to acquire?

Now for each executive on your team assess the following:

1. Can he or she rapidly grow in place?
2. Does he or she need support to stretch and grow?
3. Is he or she mismatched (a blocker or unlikely to scale)?

Step Four: Develop a Plan to Leapfrog to Your Future World

To develop a plan to leapfrog into your future world, you need to address the various situations you find yourself in with your executives.

Grow in Place Executives

Take these executives who can rapidly grow in place and share with them the expectations of how you see their role and the company growing, what you need from them, and how they can accelerate their impact. These are the leaders that many CEOs spend the least time with when, in fact, they should be spending the most. The return on effort of spending your energy and time with these executives is astronomical.

Need Support Executives

Be clear on what support these executives need. Is it context, skill building, technical ability, or personal development? Create simple, clear development goals and communicate them concisely. Dr. Martin Seligman's research on positive psychology proves that focusing on someone's strengths is far more productive than trying to fix their weaknesses, so don't waste your energy. What do they need on their team to complement their strengths? What support can you give them in mentoring or is there a coach who can help them specifically make progress against their goals?

Mismatched Executives

I have never met an executive who has regretted acting too fast. Too often a leader will say to me, if only I had acted six months ago, I would have saved all of that time, prevented others from quitting, and gotten better business results. You know who these people are. Ask yourself if they are critical to long- or short-term projects and how you can redesign their job so it plays to their strengths. If that isn't possible, create an exit plan for them.

Step Five: Redefine Today's Roles for Tomorrow

Finally, scope your roles on your executive team so they are targeted for the size and scale of your future company. If you have a VP of sales and your current revenues are $2 billion and you will grow to $6 billion in two years, hire someone who has experience managing a $6–10 billion sales organization. That is the fastest way to catapult your growth. Do this for every role (see Figure 9.1).

When Don Mattrick was appointed as CEO of Xbox in 2007, Xbox was fast becoming the runt of the Microsoft litter. While teenage boys in North America loved Xbox, it was a problem for Microsoft. It culminated in a $1 billion write-off because of the "red-ring-of-death" quality problems, and the fact that Nintendo's Wii had become the must-have toy of the moment. We were in danger of becoming irrelevant unless we broke away from our strict focus on North American males age 16–22 who liked shooting and racing games.

I was running the leadership and organization development for the Xbox division, and in Don's first week I shared some of my views on the leadership team and the changes that needed to happen for us to turn around the business. He said, "Let's spend a day on this next week." I went

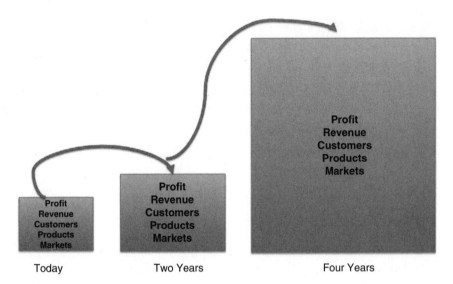

Figure 9.1 The Leapfrog Effect

to his home in Vancouver, Canada, and we talked for a day about how the business would grow in the next three years and what the implications would be for the leadership and organization. We created a plan for what we would change when. That became the basis for the three-year plan for the Xbox business.

It would be easy to stop here—many CEOs and executives do. They talk about the theory that the VP of operations needs more global experience, but they don't act on it. They know that the president of the European office is in the biggest job of his life and unlikely to succeed without additional support, but they fail to give direct, specific feedback and provide specialist help to learn new skills or change behavior. Don't be like them. Now that you have identified the gaps in your leapfrog organization, develop a plan to get you there. This has to be the number one priority of your CEO and board if you truly want to build an innovative company.

Every day you spend with a mismatched executive in a role, or settling for the people you have in place, is a day you could have spent hiring a replacement or benefiting from someone with a grander vision, greater insights, or a higher capacity for growth. Leapfrog organizations are a perpetual machine. Once you create one at the top of your organization, it cascades throughout your business with ease. It will bring up the question that is whispered in hallways more than it is talked about in boardrooms: Who will be our next CEO?

THE INTENTIONAL ANNOYANCE PHASE

Do you care what your employees think of you? Thoughtfully ruthless leaders know when to care and when to ignore their employees. When Don Mattrick joined Xbox, he refused to spend any time with anyone other than his immediate leadership team, his boss, Robbie Bach, our CEO Steve Ballmer, and perhaps specific engineering or creative leaders on specific initiatives. It would usually be one on one, or in a team meeting, but never larger crowds. Yet he was leading a 3,000-person organization that was dehydrated for information, context, and inspiration. I tried a few times to convince him to meet with groups of general managers to provide guidance on his insights and strategy, and to take questions. He refused. Every time. I realize now he was managing through the *Intentional Annoyance Stage* of rapid growth. Conventional wisdom says during change that you should speak at length and frequently to people impacted by the change, but actually the complete opposite is true. Sometimes silence is golden. The intentional annoyance phase is when you know there is going to be change, but you don't yet know what it means, or how everyone will be affected. We knew we had to make changes in Xbox to succeed, but we didn't know what those changes were yet. We knew we had ginormous gaps in our ability to beat Nintendo and Sony, but we didn't yet know how or if we would be successful. We had the secretive Project Natal as a need-to-know only project, which was the secret that we needed the organization to rally behind, but we couldn't go all out and talk about it broadly because Microsoft at the time was not the best at keeping secrets. So we rode out the intentional annoyance phase as Don continued to be thoughtfully ruthless with his time and energy.

To understand how to effectively move through the intentional annoyance phase, you can follow the Change Reaction Tool pictured in Figure 9.2.

There are two primary factors for leading your team through change in a thoughtfully ruthless way: you have to influence the level of understanding and the level of belief of your team. But first it has to start with you. Think of a change you are currently working through, and then take a look at the

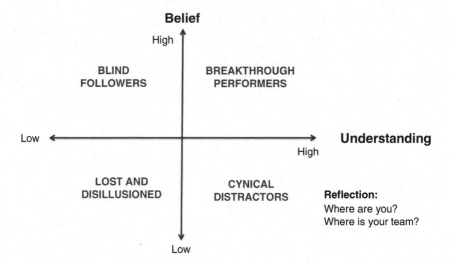

Figure 9.2 Leading Change Reactions
© Val Wright Consulting. All rights reserved.

change reaction tool. Start by rating your understanding of what is changing: Do you fully understand what is changing and why? Many times this is not clear, and this can cause the greatest amount of confusion. (In the absence of information people often make things up. They don't do it maliciously; they do it to try to make sense out of things, but that may lead to more confusion.) Once you have rated your understanding, now rate your belief in the change that is happening.

Of course your team also has to understand and believe in the change. There are four typical reactions to change. Take a look at these following descriptions of each reaction and consider where each of your team members fits:

1. Blind followers

    While it is unusual to gain followership from someone who doesn't understand, it does happen. You will hear someone say, "She has drunk the company Kool-aid." Your blind followers will follow you even if they don't fully understand where you are going.

    Corrective action: Capture that reckless enthusiasm and help them understand where you are going. Once your blind followers fully understand, they will become advocates for what you are trying to change.

2. Lost and disillusioned

Those who neither believe nor understand will be lost and disillusioned. When you have someone on your team like this, it is highly likely they will quit, which may be the right decision for you and the employee, but often this is not a conscious decision.

Corrective action: Start with helping make sure your employee understands the changes. You can't easily make someone believe if they don't understand.

3. Cynical distractors

The hardest people to influence are cynical distractors, those on your team who fully understand what you are trying to change, but don't believe and have no desire to participate. Too many leaders take this reaction personally, which is the worst stance you can take. The key is to get curious.

Corrective action: Start with asking one simple question—why? You may have to repeat this question multiple times. I used to have someone on my team who firmly did not believe in the changes that I was implementing, moving our team from focusing on volume and activity to smaller focused strategic projects. He fully understood the changes I was making, and why I was making them. I eventually sat down with him and asked him multiple times why he didn't believe it was the right decision and direction. He eventually admitted that he preferred the busy, high-volume activity of our previous work, and he didn't want to work more strategically advising and influencing; he was an executor who took pride in implementation. Once I knew that, it was clear he was no longer a fit for my team and worked to transfer him to another function, where his role was focused on what he valued and what he was great at.

4. Breakthrough performers

The aspirational goal is to have your employees fully understand the change and fully believe in it. This is how you create breakthrough performers. Your ultimate goal is to move all of your team into the top right-hand corner, but don't stop there. This is a dynamic filter that can fast change; having the right mechanisms for knowing where your team and organization are is critical to rapidly developing your team.

Stabilizing action: Don't ignore these performers on your team. Use them to create contagious understanding and belief. Get them to share their stories and understanding.

Of course, when you are in the Intentional Annoyance Stage, it is permissible to know where your team is and consciously do absolutely nothing about it. This is what Don Mattrick decided to do while we were still in stealth mode with the new Kinect camera, which was under wraps as the secretive project named Natal.

Rapid growth calls for decisions that may not make you the most likeable, but sometimes silence is the best response until you have something to say.

BUILDING AN EXEMPLARY BOARD

Many CEOs forget to look upwards as they evaluate how to accelerate the growth of their company, but this can pivotally affect how fast a company can accelerate growth. How thoughtfully ruthless you are in selecting, managing, and evolving your board can make the difference between rapid growth and sluggish performance.

The biggest challenge is determining whether your board is succeeding. Results alone don't tell the full story; in fact, results can obscure the true issues that may be holding the company back. Many boards focus purely on results and governance but forget to focus on their processes, behaviors, and the five crucial elements outlined next (see Figure 9.3).

1. Talent

   It may sound obvious, but if you don't have the right CEO or a board with the right mix of experience and skills, then the rest will be futile. With the average tenure of CEOs being 3.7 years, it gives little time for performance and planning for your CEO successor. Consider where you want to expand and grow in the next five years and determine what expertise and knowledge would help accelerate that growth. One company I was working with was rapidly expanding in Europe but had no international expertise on their current board, so they quickly established a small advisory board to provide advice on the expansion, rather than wait a further year to add additional board members.

Figure 9.3 The Exemplary Board
© Val Wright Consulting. All rights reserved.

2. Leadership Pipeline

When Jim Singel, founder of Costco, stepped down, he had his successor primed and waiting in the wings. I asked him what advice he gave Craig Jelinek as he handed over the company to him, and he said he told him, "Don't screw it up." But behind the humor was a thoughtful, planned transition. Not all handovers are that successful. Building and maintaining a strong pipeline of leaders for the board and executive team is the top priority for any board. How strong is your pipeline? Is that a topic regularly discussed during your board meetings?

3. Intentional Engagement

There are many people who sit in board meetings with their eyes glazed over, just going through the routine like a tired puppet show. It is not enough to have your board members simply show up for meetings. How they behave as a group and individually will determine how functional your board really is. One of the greatest impacts a board can have is opening doors and making connections. I have seen board members identify mentors for CEOs, make introductions that led to billion-dollar acquisitions, and pave the way for exploring technical innovations and partnerships. How well is your board making those connections for you today?

4. Strategic Clarity

I have sat through too many board meetings in which the majority of time is spent on current quarter results, current customers, and operational issues. That is not the role of an exemplary board—it is the role of the CEO and executive team. An exemplary board focuses on the horizon over the next one to three years and explores strategic possibilities and partnerships; it should not function like a band of mini-CEOs focusing on immediate business. Where did you spend most of the time at your last board meeting?

5. Governance

With disastrous examples of Volkswagen, General Motors, and United Airlines all disappointing shareholders and customers with poor decisions and absent oversight, the role of board governance should be receiving a brighter spotlight than ever before.

Seven Critical Exemplary Board Processes

Focusing on results alone will not generate optimal results for your company; you also need exemplary processes and behaviors. Here are seven critical processes for an exemplary board:

1. Strategy refresh every year

One CEO of a retail company told me they have strategy discussions every three months. This not only drives their whole board crazy, but it also shows that their strategy is not solid enough to begin with. A strategy can't be set and ignored for three years, but if you are having strategy resets every three months, you likely had the wrong strategy to begin with. Refresh your strategy and make course corrections each year.

2. Board exposure to key senior talent

Too many boards operate in a secret vacuum and only appear in formal meetings and meet the team when they are presenting. Use your board to connect with and inspire your top talent.

3. Succession plan discussion twice a year

Having a conversation about who is on the succession plan and what gaps they need to close to get there is an essential part of the board's role.

4. Individual one-on-one connections

Coordinating and booking board meetings is the equivalent of trying to get ten excited puppies to all sit and shake a paw at the same time in perfect harmony, it is pretty impossible without rigor and a ruthless schedule. Given this, one-on-one connections between board members separately and with the CEO are crucial. Too often connections happen only during the meetings or hurriedly arranged dinners the night before or after a board meeting. Prioritize regular one-on-one connections that are not simply to get buy-in ahead of time for an initiative but to explore the possibilities of rapid growth.

5. One-year executive launch plan for new CEO and new board members

It takes a full year for any new CEO to fully become productive in his or her new role; rarely do CEOs get structured support for the full year. Board members even less so. Rapidly increase the time to full productivity for your CEO and for board members so they can contribute faster and more effectively.

6. Meaningful meetings

"I can't wait for my next board meeting. I will be inspired and challenged, and we'll debate direction, insights, and new ideas," said a CEO to me recently. This is fully covered in Chapter 6, and many board meetings fall foul of the same distractions and errors of other executive meetings. I was working with a recently appointed CEO who was planning to fly to the other side of the world for a three-day board meeting. He was unclear about the meeting's purpose, wasn't sure what decisions were being made, and was certain that the rest of the board were making crucial decisions prior to his arrival. Before he boarded his flight we identified how he could create agreement for establishing the way he would work with the board, where they would add individual and group expertise, and who he would target to bring into his inner circle for advice. He returned home with a clear agreement about how the board would make decisions as well as provide feedback and expertise.

Here is a fast guide for you to assess how meaningful your board meetings are:

- You are intentional about how and when you engage as a board. See the discussion in Chapter 5 about focusing on the right spot.
- Always be clear about what is going on: informing, deciding, advising, or agreeing.
- Always be the deliverer of bad news; there should be no surprises.
- Instill meeting discipline in this way by adhering to these parameters:
  - A clear purpose
  - Inclusive participation
  - Use of a facilitator (if necessary) to build your meeting muscles
  - Leverage open space of free time with no agenda for real-time discussion
  - An understand of company/country culture differences
  - Agreement about how you will disagree

7. Annual CEO and Board Performance Evaluations

   For all the time and effort involved in often-futile performance reviews of employees, the most crucial evaluations often get skipped. A critical role of the board is to evaluate their CEO and themselves. One CEO recently shared with me he only knows he is performing adequately if he survives just one more board meeting without getting fired. That is like trying to play archery blindfolded—too much luck and a high probability someone will get hurt!

The final area of an exemplary board is the crucial behaviors that every board member needs to exemplify:

1. Candid
2. Transparent
3. Thoughtfully ruthless
4. Mutual respect
5. Crystal-clear communication
6. Proactive
7. Flexible backbone
8. Self-aware
9. Fully engaged

Finally, whether you are a board member, CEO, or an executive presenting to your board, here are seven powerful questions to expect your board to ask if you are to be thoughtfully ruthless:

1. Who is your successor and what is your successor action plan?
2. How is your executive team performing?
3. What unexpected competitors do you anticipate?
4. What is your view on the risks we are taking in our investments?
5. What trends do you predict in our industry next year?
6. How confident are you in our return on investment?
7. How strong is your pipeline for innovation?

Your exemplary board has a profound impact on how you can create a leapfrog organization by holding you accountable, bringing fresh perspectives, and inspiring your whole executive team.

LEAVING YOUR LEGACY

The final aspect of creating a leapfrog organization is leaving your legacy. Do you know how you will be remembered long after you have left? Have you even considered it?

Steve Jobs left one of the most profound legacies a leader has ever created: Movies, books, and expert assessments and insights. What most agree on is that Jobs was not likeable, nor did he want to be, but the most poignant aspect of Jobs was the legacy he set out to leave through his relentless pursuit of innovation.

When Ali Brown was due to go out with friends after work one evening, she went to the ATM and couldn't withdraw any cash because she only had $18.76 in her account. She had to call her friends and cancel their night out. It was at that very moment that Ali knew she was going to change her fortunes and leave a legacy; she just didn't quite know what it was yet. Ali began with an e-mail newsletter, which turned into selling short e-books and advice, which turned into an online following of a million. She has since appeared on *Secret Millionaire*, won awards for philanthropic efforts supporting women, and was invited by Richard Branson to his British Virgin Island retreat as part of his entrepreneurs philanthropic retreat. Her legacy is in place, yet still she reinvents herself and her business.

To be thoughtfully ruthless with your resources, you have to know and outwardly articulate the legacy you want to leave—and develop a plan that allows you to achieve it.

Here is how to take your wishful thinking to reality:

The Wishful Thinking Wonder List

1. Give yourself 30 minutes of uninterrupted silence with a pen and paper.
2. Dream. With no buts and no if-onlys.
3. Write for 30 minutes. Don't stop until 30 minutes is up.
4. Write a letter to yourself of your greatest hopes for the impact you want to have—include home, work, community, family, people, and life in general.
5. Don't have caveats. Write fast and don't go back and edit.
6. After 30 minutes stop and go outside. Walk, run, play with your dogs, take a gym class, or lift weights. Just do anything physical and away from your office, desk, or home.
7. Leave your writing alone for some period of time—an hour, a full day, whatever you choose.
8. Decide who you want to share your writing with: a trusted advisor, your mentor, a family member.
9. Ask them to listen first, and then ask you questions.
10. Now discuss how you can make these things happen. What is the first step you can take?
11. Repeat with step two, adjust, and repeat with step three.

The fastest way to accelerate a plan to make your wishful thinking a reality is to share it with someone you trust, so step 8 is the most pivotal step.

By addressing each of the elements discussed in this chapter, you can assess and plan for every aspect of your organization. This will help you to create a leapfrog organization that will force you to be thoughtfully ruthless with your resources.

Chapter 10

THE THOUGHTFULLY RUTHLESS TEAM

As a steeplechase racehorse on the British racetrack bursts out of the gate with maximum speed, you know there are challenging jumps and obstacles ahead, but what if you were to eliminate the fences all together? Then, there would be a clear path to the finish line. Similarly, a team that invests time to learn how to run straight rather than wasting energy on leaping each fence will catapult ahead of their competition.

Successful leaders know how to sequence their focus for galvanizing their teams. It's not uncommon for sequencing to get out of order here. Many leaders start with team-building activities when they haven't considered where their business is and how they want it to grow, and therefore, they start team building with the wrong team. This chapter outlines common scenarios, the right sequencing, and how to assess and act on galvanizing your team in a thoughtfully ruthless way. Practical exercises are included to use for improving decision making, banishing mediocrity, creating inspiring communication, and providing crystal-clear feedback.

These are common scenarios that business leaders face:

- Your business is growing at warp speed, and the leaders and organizations can't keep up.
- Too much leadership time is spent on executing current opportunities versus considering potential new opportunities and making strategic choices.

- Your employees and decisions are not aligned with the needs of your customers.
- Innovation is slower than your competition.
- A communication bubble exists around the leaders or leadership team; like oil and water the two versions of the truth repel each other.
- Decisions are not clear, may not stick, take too long, or get made and then undone.
- Your competition and your industry are evolving at a faster rate than you are, and you need reinvention.
- Multiple changes have occurred creating confusion, misalignment, and misdirected effort.
- A new leader or team member has created uncertainty and lack of clarity.
- Individuals and teams are not running at maximum efficiency and fail to be thoughtfully ruthless with their time, energy, and resources.

All of these situations can be accelerated or decelerated by how galvanized the leadership team is.

Earlier in my career I had a strong belief that leaders were delusional about their teams' performance. I thought they couldn't see what I could see, as if they had an obscure filter on their business glasses or they were just slightly blind to the evidence I could observe. I soon realized I was the one who was wrong. Leaders aren't delusional as they look at their teams, nor do their abilities correlate to a personality type assessed by some invalid test that tells them they are a "D-leader," a purple-squirrel, or a green giraffe, meaning they need to lead their team in a certain way.

What I realized is that certain situations cause leaders to act in a certain way that makes them appear a bit delusional. Here are five of the most common distractors that prevent leaders from realizing they need to galvanize their team:

1. Frantic—A leader can become frantic when she is too busy solving the burning issue of the day to stop and pay attention to what is happening within her team. She may have a misguided belief that powering through execution is more valuable. This occurs in fast-growing businesses in which rapid growth overtakes planning and reflection.

2. Hopeful—Eventually that poor performer will leave, won't they? It is easy to become hopeful just like the rookie golf player, hoping he can play at St. Andrews without being spotted as a newcomer to the game. Optimism is essential, but blind hope is catastrophic for your team.

3. Impatient—You told them once, they have your goals, and they are senior enough to figure it out for themselves. A leader who becomes impatient can be the equivalent of an automatic tennis ball machine firing serves in every direction without giving anyone time to return the first serve back. Finding the right pace for your team is critical to galvanizing them.

4. Skeptical—I have worked with leaders who saw no value in bringing their team together beyond fast, functional, tactical monthly meetings. Their belief was they have products to ship, customers to support, and goals to execute, and any time spent together as a team is a superfluous distraction.

5. Lost—This is the one situation that can be the hardest to detect, especially if you live in a world of high bravado and low vulnerability. If you know a leader that is in the biggest job of his or her life, then you know it is easy to become overwhelmed and freeze.

These are not personality types; they are situational reactions and you can experience more than one in parallel. The critical first step is to notice where you are and acknowledge it so you can focus on how you are galvanizing your team while growing your business. Consider which resonates most with you as you read the rest of this chapter.

In my quarter of a century of corporate and consulting life, I must have experienced more than $5 million worth of team development activities. Some were painful, some hilarious, some pointless, some embarrassing, and some outrageous fun, but they all had one common trait: completely futile in their ability to actually improve how the team accelerated results. You can decide which falls into which category (names and companies have been withheld to protect the innocent):

- Running around London on a treasure hunt while tied to two colleagues I had never met before.
- Flying to a private island by seaplane.
- Climbing trees 100 feet high and crossing rope bridges.
- Given two hours to create a short film.

- Fly fishing on a private estate.
- Abandoned in a remote field with a compass and a GPS radio.
- A race to see which team could assemble a Land Rover Defender SUV the fastest.
- Obstacle course in a Mini.
- Mud run at night.
- Creating a unique piece of blown glass.

I could go on, and I am sure you could add your own. I have been on both sides of the table when executives and well-intentioned human resources experts were trying to create fun, naively assuming that a game of bowls will make the team happier and more bonded when the complete opposite is true.

I am not advising against fun—far from it. But fun cannot be the sole focus of your bringing your team together, and it cannot replace the fundamental foundation of a galvanized team. Many leaders hope that a team-building event will improve morale. But who wants to spend time bowling with their coworkers or learning about your preferred communication style if your strategy isn't clear, you are missing opportunities to grow your business, or there is a toxic leader on your team not being dealt with? Don't waste your money. Not yet.

STEPS FOR GALVANIZING YOUR TEAM

The secret is all in the sequencing. Here are the nine crucial first steps to galvanizing your team:

1. Stop all leadership team development.

    This one surprises leaders the most when they contact me to ask for help building their team. You have to first stop and take a genuine pause until you know you have the team that is going to lead your business for the next three years. Any investment in team building or leadership alignment is futile if you lack confidence that your team is the right team for the future. I have watched senior executives spend days in retreats trying to resolve disagreements on strategy, tactics, and people when in reality the leader knows one of those individuals won't be on the team in a couple of months. When the axe finally falls and the person is off the team, you have wasted all of that time and energy because the dynamic of the team is completely changed. Save energy, time, and money by delaying those retreats, off-sites, and meetings until you have the right team in place. Then take swift action.

2. Pay attention to what you are rewarding.

This is the largest disconnect in most companies. Companies reward individual performance, yet ask for teamwork and sharing. Do your words match how you recognize and reward your employees? True teamwork happens when a team has shared goals, shared results, and shared financial success. Very few companies truly offer that; yet, they expect team members to act like they are a team. Changing your rewards and recognition programs in parallel with galvanizing your team will mean you are rewarding what you are asking your team to change, which will increase your probability of success.

3. Establish shared goals.

When House of Fraser opened a new store in Swindon, England, it was their first store opening for the department store group in more than eight years. The regional director added to the objectives of all 11 regional stores that a successful store launch in Swindon was a shared goal of the region. This meant that it wasn't just the responsibility of the Swindon store management team to launch the store on time, but every store manager had a vested interest in its success. Other stores were willing to loan key visual merchandising people for the launch, help with training new teams, and be there on launch day to make sure everything ran smoothly. Had those shared goals not been established, the offers of help and support may not have been so fast and furious.

Get clear on where you want your team to work together and where you want them to act independently. This will inform where the team will be rewarded for results beyond their individual responsibilities.

4. Look ahead three years and build that team now.

Chapter 9 outlined how to build your leapfrog organization. Repositioning and hiring your leadership team should be your number one priority until your team is in place. Putting that team in place will accelerate your impact and reduce your stress dramatically.

5. Set your team up for success.

When a leader takes on a new role, the more senior he is, the higher the likelihood that he will be thrown into the deep end and expected to figure out his new role for himself. If you have new leaders on your team, increase their probability of success by giving them a clear plan for getting onboard; set expectations and spend 50 percent of your time with them for the first month.

6. Boundaries, goals, and expectations.

Leaders who have an open, trusting relationship with their boss deliver results faster and take bold moves to grow the business. Help everyone by proactively having the "so how do you like to work?" conversation. Share with your team what makes you happy and what drives you crazy and ask them to reciprocate. Don't wait until conflict or misunderstanding arises; do it now.

7. Energy is spent on customers and increasing profits, not on internal drama.

Successful leaders create organizations that do not rely on them, because they empower others. They create tenets that give leaders guidelines to make decisions by. They decide how they are going to make the decision, communicate it, and move on. There is no distraction or energy invested in internal drama, conflict, or confusion. Simple.

8. Ensure your leaders are absorbing and amplifying the right points.

Ambiguity and confusion can be accelerated or decelerated by leaders throughout your company. Ensure that your leaders have time for hearing directly from you and give them opportunity to air concerns and questions. You need leaders who can absorb the friction and emotion while amplifying key important messages that may impact customers or profits.

9. Take 10 percent of your time and invest in your leaders of tomorrow.

Exceptional leaders personally know the highest performers with the greatest potential in each of their critical disciplines. You owe it to them to spend 10 percent of your week, every week, growing them, developing them, and setting an example to your leaders on how to invest in your leaders of the future. This gives your organization the gift of a strong pipeline of leaders and experts for the future.

Once your team is in place, then and only then is it time to assess where your team is and build a plan to galvanize your team. You can start with the following assessment.

The Galvanized Leadership Team

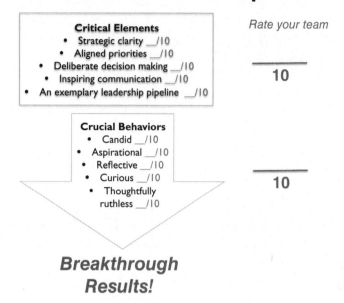

Rate your team

Critical Elements
- Strategic clarity __/10
- Aligned priorities __/10
- Deliberate decision making __/10
- Inspiring communication __/10
- An exemplary leadership pipeline __/10

10

Crucial Behaviors
- Candid __/10
- Aspirational __/10
- Reflective __/10
- Curious __/10
- Thoughtfully ruthless __/10

10

Breakthrough Results!

Figure 10.1 Galvanize Your Team Assessment
Use the galvanize your team assessment to assess where your team is.

Galvanize Your Team Assessment

Rate your team using a scale of 1–10 with 10 being the highest for each of the critical elements and crucial behaviors (see Figure 10.1).

Complete this yourself for your team, but you can also ask your team to complete its assessment. I use this when I work with executive teams, and the results give me insight into where the team has the greatest strengths to build on. It is the hardest part for any leader or team when they see an assessment like this. Immediately they want to talk about their gaps, their weakness, and what they need to fix, when in reality the greatest opportunity the assessment presents is discovering how to leverage their strength as a team. Positive psychologist Dr. Martin Seligman advises that the greatest way to feel inspired to work on what you don't want to work on is to leverage your strengths in areas where you are not so strong.

THE CHARACTERISTICS OF A GALVANIZED TEAM

A galvanized team is an active team, on the move and working toward a shared goal. Committed. Passionate. Working in sync. We'll take a look here at the elements and behaviors that indicate a team is galvanized and setting themselves up for success.

Five Critical Elements of a Galvanized Team

1. Strategic clarity—Everyone on your team is clear on the future direction of two or three years and how you will get there.
2. Aligned priorities—Your priorities individually and as a team are clear.
3. Deliberate decision making—Everyone understands who makes what decisions, and the outcomes are clear to everyone.
4. Inspiring communication—Everyone across your organization hears multiple ways and multiple messages at the right time to inspire and guide decisions.
5. Exemplary leadership pipeline—There is an abundance of available talent to take on the next level of leadership and expertise roles, and proactive planning takes place.

Five Crucial Behaviors of a Galvanized Team

1. Candid—Everyone is comfortable saying what they think with positive intentions.
2. Aspirational—There is a common future focus and optimistic view of the future.
3. Curious—When an opinion or fact is counter to your own, you seek to understand before reaching a conclusion.
4. Reflective—As a team you create time and space to reflect on successes and understand why you were successful as well as why it didn't go according to plan.
5. Thoughtfully ruthless—As a team you are deliberate and intentional about where you spend the team's time and energy and the collective resources of the whole organization.

Deliberate Decision Making Matters

Of the hundreds of teams I have worked with, a lack of deliberate decision making is the number one cause of wasted energy and wasted time in teams (see Figure 10.2).

Cautious to risk ←———————————→ Embraces risk

Solo ←———————————→ Consensus

Decide and un-decide ←———————————→ Decide and it sticks

Data and analysis ←———————————→ Gut

Fast ←———————————→ Slow

Reflection:
Plot your preference
Plot your manager's preference
Plot the cultural norm

Figure 10.2   The Decision Dilemma

Chapter 11 further explores Amazon's culture, and its decision-making culture is one of the clearest I have ever witnessed. Even as Amazon made thousands of new hires each year, it was crystal clear how decisions were made. When companies are in rapid growth, it can be hard to press pause and stop to outline how decisions are made; many leaders are not even conscious of how they make decisions. When I invite leaders to write a *top-ten decision-making tenets* list for their teams, some struggle until they see the decision-making dilemma continuum; that is when they see their preferred decision-making style and how it impacts others. Successful leaders are ruthless not just with their own time but also with their team's time. Refer to Chapter 6 for more about creating impactful meetings, although a meet-and-decide culture goes beyond formal meetings. Regularly ask your team to share how you can help unlock decisions and remove roadblocks to faster decisions further down in your organization. Lead by example and create spontaneous decision points in which you encourage real-time gathering of the relevant people to make decisions that are time sensitive.

First a warning: This is not a method to change how you make decisions. Remember when you last made a major purchase, like a house or a car. Think back to how you made that decision. Did you research reviews and comparison shop for hours? Did you walk into the showroom or open house and say, "I will take that one" and decide immediately? Did you make a decision, but then talk to others and then update your decision in a different direction? Did you keep your decision quiet and make it on your own, or ask other people you trusted?

How you make decisions is unlikely to change, and you are unlikely to change the decision-making preference of your team, your boss, and your peers. The crucial step is understanding.

Plot yourself on the decision dilemma continuum, and then plot where you predict your boss is, along with the cultural norm of your division or company.

This is one of my most favorite exercises I run with teams. I first ask people to plot this privately and then come up and plot it on a whiteboard. It only takes a few minutes before someone shouts, "Oh, now I understand you!" or "Oh, how tough it must be for Stacy right over on the other side of all of the rest of us."

Looking at the sample team in Figure 10.3, answer the following questions:

1. What observations do you notice with this team?
2. What do you think you would observe as this team makes decisions?
3. Who do you think will expend the most energy and time with decision making?
4. What steps could the team take to help more deliberate decision making?

There is a big "it depends" when identifying how to improve a team's deliberate decision making. You have to factor in the typical decision making for the division or company and where the boss is relative to their

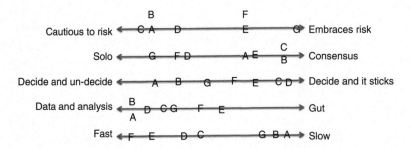

Figure 10.3　Sample Decision Dilemma Continuum

team. This is why it is a tremendous help to the team when the leader creates a "Top Ten Decision-Making Tenets"; it helps the team know how to work together.

Surprise Bonus   As a bonus for readers, I am making a special offer here for the first 20 readers who e-mail me their team's *galvanize your team* scores along with their team's *decision-making dilemma team profile*. I will review it for you as a special gift and provide guidance on how you can improve your decision making within your team. E-mail me at val@valwrightconsulting.com.

Inspiring Communication

The other area where I have found teams want the most help for new and innovative ideas is how to provide inspiring communication to their teams. In the last few years, there has been a strong trend toward electronic communication; 95 percent of communication happens by e-mail or other online messaging platforms, and much of it is tedious—and enough to send most readers to sleep! There is inspiration all around us; yet, many leaders revert to fact-based communication of numbers and product information, resulting in data overload. Banksy is a British street artist who is as famous as he is mysterious, with treasure hunts, exclusive interviews, and hoax arrest reports. Banksy creates excitement and provokes thought. His month-long art installation, *Better Out Than In*, in New York revealed a new art installation every day. It became a treasure hunt, shared on social media, creating excitement and conversation about controversial topics. In a *Village Magazine* interview, Banksy said he wanted to keep people looking at his artwork for as long as possible. He was shocked by a British museum study that revealed that visitors only looked at paintings for an average of eight seconds. So he accompanied his New York installations with a museum-style audio guide that you could reach by calling a telephone number to hear more about his piece of art. It was attention grabbing, impactful, and innovative. Leaders need to consider how you can communicate differently to capture the attention in eight seconds or less.

Here are some unusual and imaginative ways you can inspire your team:

1. Tell a Story
   "I will always remember . . ." or "I wish you could have seen . . ."
   These phrases are memorable and capture imagination and excitement. Try it in your next meeting or talk.

2. Capture a Raw Video

This can work because it's different. Use your phone and record a simple video message, sharing what is currently important to you or providing a fast update after a customer visit or board meeting. This works great from a conference room floor or on a customer site visit. The raw unedited versions work best.

3. Share Why *You* Are Really Excited

Is it your products, your future plan for expansion, or the latest customer feedback? Excitement is addictive—share it with your team today.

4. Remember One Thing

Don't overload your messages. Before you send any communication, think about what is the one point you want everyone to remember and make sure you make that clearly.

5. Cut the Small Talk

Jump right into the message, especially when you're speaking in meetings or in front of groups. Don't ramble about microphones, the weather, or what day of the week it is.

6. Share a Picture

Variety catches attention. Try using a picture to capture and communicate one of your ideas.

7. Forget PowerPoint

It is hard to inspire via bulleted text. Don't do it unless it contains just a few pictures. Speak naturally to capture attention.

8. Avoid Lengthy E-mails

Get your people out of their in-boxes. Experiment with e-mails that are short and to the point.

9. Watch Your Tone

Have you heard yourself lately? Are *you* energized and inspired? Either way, it is contagious.

10. Share a Song

I once had a boss who started every meeting with a quote from a song. It was a little silly perhaps, but it was memorable, and it got everyone talking about his message.

11. Remember News Clippings?

If you see a powerful article in a magazine or in the *Wall Street Journal*, share it old-school style. Different stands out.

12. Be Okay with Messy

    Don't spend hours perfecting your talk, your e-mail, or your meeting. Teach your team that messy can be great and perfection isn't often worth the investment of time.

13. Talk about Five Years into the Future

    If your team does not know the destination, how can they enjoy the journey?

14. Surprise Them: Do the Opposite of What They Expect

    Do you always hold large all-employee meetings? Try small-group breakfasts. Experiment with different ways of inspiring your team and find out what works best for you and them.

15. Make It Personal

    Do your team and company know who you are? What stories can you share about your early career, your personal passions, and how you became the leader you are? The more authentic you are, the greater connection you create.

16. Listen to Yourself

    When did you last play back a recording or video of yourself? It is a powerful way to hear if your intent matches reality. Have the courage to assess your speaking impact and strengthen it. Get help from a coach if you cringe as you listen.

17. Do You Understand and Believe?

    To be inspired you have to both understand and believe in the company direction. Before you inspire your team, you have to make sure you understand and believe yourself.

Inspiring leaders experiment with new approaches, ask for feedback about their communication, and develop new skills as they grow in their career and take on new opportunities that put them in front of larger crowds or more challenging audiences.

The Most Crucial Behavior of All

While all of the five crucial behaviors are important, the strongest differentiator of outstanding performance is when a team demonstrates curiosity. Curiosity can be observed when you watch how someone reacts to a view that opposes their own.

What do you do when you discover evidence that one of your strong opinions may not, in fact, be entirely correct? How do you handle it when your new product launch doesn't go as planned or your competition jumps ahead of you? Many leaders shut down, start a furious debate, venomously disagree, or get defensive. Curiosity is a better response. It gives you the gift of exploration without judgment; yet, it is hard to master if it doesn't come naturally to you.

Waiting before responding will help you think about being more curious. By pausing before jumping in, you will give yourself time to think about your response. If you also pay attention to how you feel, it will help you identify whether you need to stop and get curious. If you are frustrated, annoyed, impatient, or angry, ask yourself why. Do that first— before you ask why someone holds a different opinion from yours. Then, when you are hearing their response about why they hold their opinion, you can stop to really listen and seek to understand their point of view by asking, "Why do you believe that?" or "Why did you come to that conclusion?" Keep asking why until you understand.

The more senior you get in your career, the less likely it becomes that people will disagree with you. A trick to use that gives people permission to disagree with you is to state your opinion and then ask who has a different point of view. In this way, the different point of view can be looked at as just that—different—rather than as a disagreement. The label is subtle but important because it is easier to say, "I see it differently" than "I disagree with you."

I have witnessed the most remarkable discussions when there is disruptive disagreement. You can set the tone for tolerating disagreement in a very productive way. By remaining curious without trying to enter into a battle, you can gain incredible insights by listening to the different points of view. Some companies do not want disagreement in public, only in private. This makes for challenging decision making because it slows everything down to a treacle pace. Encouraging productive and meaningful disagreement teaches others what is important to you and that it is acceptable to speak your mind and not hold back.

I used to work with a regional leader who would regularly ask his peers about their regions. He barraged them with questions about their business, their sales, and their growth plans. He frustrated everyone he met because they thought his questions meant he doubted their ability to deliver on their quarterly projections and that he was acting superior. When I spoke with him about it, he told me he had heard that their regions were outperforming his own, and he wanted to learn why they were so successful. I told him he needed to share the intention behind his questions because his questioning style was putting people off and confusing them. Once he did this, his interactions were far more productive, and his peers began volunteering more information and became more open to sharing ideas with him. Might others doubt your intentions and is that clouding your ability to be curious?

Here are three fast ways you can adopt the curiosity mind-set today:

1. Analyze your successes. Then identify how you can rapidly replicate them.
2. Listen to those you have recently hired. Consider how you can leverage their unique talents and abilities.
3. Gather five of your most contrarian employees and invite them to a discussion about your current vision and strategy. Ask them what is holding it back, how you can accelerate growth, and what you personally can do as a leader to improve the probability of success.

When your team sees you getting curious, it becomes contagious!

DO YOU TOLERATE MEDIOCRITY?

I was speaking at a conference, and at the end, a CEO approached me and said, "I have to work with you." A four-minute conversation and a handshake sealed us working together. Later, I asked him what had prompted such a quick decision, and he said it was during my talk when I said that the most powerful thing a CEO can do for his company is fire him or herself when the time is right. When you first think about challenging mediocrity in a company, it is easy to think of the teams and managers across the company, when sometimes it is the mediocrity tolerated by the CEO or board that needs tackling first to set the tone for the whole company. My CEO client and I created a new role for him as an advisor to the board, pinpointing where he added the most value to his company and allowing him to work on what energized and inspired him the most.

Some companies are the perfect hiding ground for underperformers; others pass around mismatched employees indefinitely. If you are not focused on outstanding performance, you are damaging your company and your own personal leadership reputation.

Here are the three biggest mistakes leaders make that inadvertently encourage mediocrity:

- Hesitating—Waiting too long to tackle mismatched employees.
- Silence—Failing to explain expectations and discuss whether employees hit or miss them.
- Reward—Inadequate recognition for great leaders of people.

You cannot accelerate growth and innovation when you tolerate mediocrity. Your highest performers will become frustrated and your own leadership reputation will become tarnished. Your highest performers may say: "How do they get away with it?" "Why doesn't their boss take action?" "Maybe this isn't the right place for me." You will create an organization that is known for being an easy ride where misfits are put out to pasture. Your underperformers will remain oblivious that they are not meeting expectations. The time spent on customers, products, and profit will reduce as energy is absorbed by drama, gossip, and unproductive conversations.

I developed this *mediocrity measurement assessment* to help companies determine their tolerance level for mediocrity.

Mediocrity Measurement Assessment

Score one point for each yes.

1. Do you set clear leadership expectations for your people managers?
2. Do you have frequent forums for people managers to discuss, to share, and to learn outstanding leadership lessons?
3. Do you hold up your strongest people managers as role models for others?
4. Do you spend 25 percent of your leadership team discussions on people topics?
5. Do you have 90-day reviews with new hires?
6. Does every employee have clear measurable goals?
7. Do employees have regular one-on-ones to discuss goals, roadblocks, and personal development?
8. Do you actively identify and manage out underperformers?
9. Do you exit underperformers swiftly, objectively, and with grace?
10. Are rewards tied to achieving goals and demonstrating your company values?

Your Mediocrity Score

10—Congratulations—Don't lose sight of those high standards you have set. You attract and retain high performers and have built a reputation for not tolerating mediocrity. Ask your leadership team to also take the assessment and see whether they agree with your perspective.

7–9—Nearly there!—You stand out from the crowd as a company that sets high standards and ensures exemplary performance. You have a few blind spots, so focus on those quickly and you will create outstanding results.

5–6—Danger Zone—You have established some great practices, but you have a number of gaps that will stall your ability to build great products and delight customers. Pay attention to what you are missing and develop a plan to accelerate changes in those areas.

< 4 Mediocrity Inc.—Watch out. If you are not losing important team members, you soon will be. You need to overhaul how you manage people in your organization. Get help, fast.

I worked with one company that had recently been taken over by a large Fortune 500 company. Their expectations of mediocrity varied greatly between the directors responsible for the largest parts of the organization, the founders, and the divisional president of the acquiring company. A year after the acquisition it was clear that there was a disconnect between what standards of performance and results were expected because, prior to the acquisition, the founders and CEO were very tolerant and forgiving if deadlines were missed and quality dropped. It wasn't long before it was agreed the CEO would leave, and we used that as a catalyst for resetting expectations for everyone who managed people in the company, which is step 1 in a four-step process to banish mediocrity.

Four Steps to Banishing Mediocrity

1. Expectations

    Let your leaders know you want them to lead! Just like the company discussed previously, you may need to press the reset button with your people managers about expectations. There may be a skill gap in your managers' ability to know how to set and maintain expectations. Share your leadership values about how you want leaders to lead in your organization.

2. Goals

Every employee should have goals at the start of your business year. Too many companies forget or wait three months to perfect them. Meanwhile employees are making decisions about where they spent their time as well as trade-offs about products and customers, all without recent direction. Too many leaders assume that employees know the latest direction in strategy or product focus, when in reality there is confusion. Don't make goals overly complex; they should be clear and easy to measure. Every manager of a team should have a people-related goal, and every senior leader should have a multiyear goal focused on the strategy.

3. Feedback

Do not treat everyone equally. Be thoughtful about the experience and style of each member of your team and adapt your feedback appropriately. Vary your frequency and depth of feedback, depending on tenure and anticipated autonomy. A recent hire, a leader of a remote team, and someone in the biggest role of their career will all have different needs for feedback. Often leaders forget to ask how people like to receive feedback and neglect to test whether it is working throughout the year. Another common error is waiting too long to share feedback, which loses both impact and relevance. If you ever find yourself telling someone else about your concerns regarding an employee's perform-ance before you have told the employee, you are likely failing to communicate feedback effectively.

4. Action

I have yet to meet a leader that has regretted taking action too fast on a misfit on their team. Be fair, reasonable, fast, and decisive when choosing your course of action. You would be remiss to ignore legal advice, but don't let this command your actions because legal experts have a duty to share all of the risks, just as you have a duty to balance that advice and make informed business decisions.

At this point, you may be convinced of the need to make changes, but your team may start to suffer from incessant excuse syndrome (IES). I have observed this with many leaders when they try to banish mediocrity. Here are the top two excuses and how to overcome them:

1. "We can't hire only superstars. That would be impossible!"

   That may be true, but consider what you have tried and why it didn't work. Set the bar high, and the energy and focus in your company will increase, rapidly. I regularly see organizations without strategic direction, employees without goals and coasting along, when it would be better for everyone if decisive action were taken. Amazon uses a distinctive test for all of their new hires: "Is this person better than 50 percent of the people doing this role today?" That is a great test to ensure you are continually raising the bar. Many times the underperformer or mismatched employee will call you three months later to thank you for ending their misery and allowing them to find a job they love.

2. "We have a busy quarter; we will launch this later."

   Every month you wait is a month in which you risk that one of your best people will quit. Solutions are neither time consuming nor complex; they just require commitment. Gather all of your employees who manage people, share your leadership values, and explain how you want them to lead. Have a conversation with your people managers about expectations and ask them what they need from you to help them raise the expectations for performance on their teams.

Only now is it time to assess your team and decide on development investments for individuals or your team. At this point, you will be building on a solid foundation, and you will see faster results because you have taken the time to raise your expectations of your team and create a sense of shared purpose. Start with a robust development plan for each of your leaders, with specific goals and measurements, and then identify who would benefit from a mentor or an external coach. Then you can assess how galvanized your team is and where your greatest investment and focus will yield the best results.

Chapter 11

AMAZON VERSUS MICROSOFT

This chapter explores the rivalry between Microsoft and Amazon and how thoughtfully ruthless both Jeff Bezos and Steve Ballmer were as CEOs of companies located six miles apart in Seattle. They fought like stubborn teenagers for talent, customers, and new market ideas; yet, the two companies are polar opposite in the way they lead, build products, and produce results. Ballmer has shaped the results of the last 10 years at Microsoft as he desperately fought against the rumors for his resignation, determined to prove Microsoft could once again be successful. Meanwhile six miles away, Bezos quietly was accelerating the growth of Amazon. These two leaders could not be more different, and this chapter explores the key differences between Bezos and Ballmer, in particular what any leader can learn from the best parts of the Amazon and Microsoft cultures.

At the Safeco Field stadium, home to Seattle's baseball team the Mariners, "Eye of the Tiger" was blaring from the speakers, and suddenly from the top of the stadium Steve Ballmer, Microsoft's CEO at the time, came sprinting through the stadium high-fiving everyone as he went. His lap of the stadium lasted for the whole of the song and by the time he got to the stage, he was dripping in sweat and out of breath. When he got there he screamed, "I LOVE THIS COMPANY!" Steve Ballmer was known for his acts of almost childlike excitement. Many company meetings he would scream himself hoarse; he once had one of those teddy bear–shaped honey bottles and would regularly stop and squirt honey into his throat so he could continue with his excited whoops and screams.

As a stereotypically reserved Brit recently relocated from England to Seattle, that first company meeting I was in complete shock and awe, not just from Ballmer's abundant energy but from the crowd itself: 20,000 strong, with custom-designed swag with logos from their division and lunchboxes of snacks, eyes hypnotized, arms waving, and everyone whooping back as if it were a rock concert. Despite the glaring absence of a conversation about the stagnant share price, the content was obsessively deep in technical showcases of the newest features in Excel or the latest upgrade to the features of PowerPoint.

Contrast that with my first experience seeing Jeff Bezos in action. We were in KeyArena West, a short walk from Amazon's headquarters in South Lake Union in downtown Seattle. Bezos quietly appeared on stage, and this was his first question to the audience: "Who is new here and this is their first Town Hall meeting?" More than half of the stadium stood up and everyone else gave them a quiet round of applause. Amazon was growing at an incredible pace, and their greatest challenge after hiring all of those new Amazonians was how to help them understand the Amazon way of how products are built, customers are obsessed over, and decisions are made. Everything revolved around the customer, every decision started with the customer and why a new feature or product would improve their lives. Bezos was curious about the competition, but more curious about what a customer needed and how Amazon could provide it. On stage, he told story after story of how Amazon's products were transforming customers' lives, and as long as we all acted with the customers' best interests in mind, we had the power, freedom, and authority to challenge and change anything.

In another company meeting, in the early years of Microsoft launching their Windows Phone, an unsuspecting employee foolishly took a picture of Ballmer using his iPhone. Ballmer saw this from the stage, went to the front row, and grabbed the phone from his hand, threw it to the ground and pretended to jump on it. Ballmer didn't take kindly to employees who used competitors' products, especially when they were superior to Microsoft's own creations. When Microsoft's first search engine launched, few people in the Redmond headquarters used it, and this infuriated Ballmer who published statistics that showed how many Microsoft employees were using rival product Google search and showed it by division across the company to try and shame employees into using Bing. In the Xbox Division, many of the VPs had iPhones and used MacBooks, proudly using them and sharing why their design and user experience was an inspiration for our own design and product teams. In the Sales Division, it was a different story; nobody could be seen with an iPhone, and when I took a new job in their Services Division, I had to buy a second phone to use during meetings and keep my iPhone hidden at the bottom of my purse.

Microsoft coined the phrase *dog-fooding* in the early nineties, meaning you were expected to eat your own dog food to test it, or in Microsoft's case use the software internally that they were selling to customers. This makes perfect sense, but sometimes there was a blind belief that any competitors' product was inferior and there was nothing to be learned from it, particularly in the ginormous divisions of Windows and Microsoft Office.

A visceral reaction to competition existed across Microsoft, which played out within the internal company culture, too. This dated back from the way Bill Gates used to drive fast innovation. He would set up three teams all with the same goal. He did this when he wanted to create a spreadsheet application. He told three different teams he wanted them to create a spreadsheet tool, and he told them there were two other teams working on the same challenge. The winning team with the best product would get to produce it and the two losing teams would be moved to work on the winning product. The motivation was to win at any cost, and not to be the losing team whose work would be wasted and having to work on a product that they weren't emotionally invested in.

That story was folklore at Microsoft. Whenever there was an internal battle between teams, often someone would tell the story about how Bill Gates had deliberately created it that way and that is how the Excel product and many others came to be.

Ballmer and Gates were ultimately prepared to break from their cultural norms when the final plans for Xbox were approved. The Xbox leadership did not want to use Windows inside the box; they wanted an operating system highly tuned for gaming and a completely separate team and campus. Being willing to create a subculture within their own gargantuan culture was one of the smartest decisions Ballmer and Gates made. Xbox would not have been born if it had been tied into Windows, either the technology or the product division. Innovation needs new ideas and thinking, and you cannot always achieve that with existing teams and existing people. Ballmer let Bach and Allard go off campus to put further distance between the Xbox team and the parent company that would fund their multibillion-dollar project. Sean Gorman, Director of Strategic Planning at Xbox got to experience that culture firsthand: "Robbie Bach, President of Entertainment and Devices at Microsoft created a distinct culture within Microsoft. Robbie always encouraged to start with the end in mind. We started with three-page strategy outline; that turned into a 30-page brief, which turned into a 300-page plan. We wrote the magazine cover story that we wanted to have for Xbox 360 before doing anything else. Amazon does the same, every new investment starts with writing the launch press release as step one. Then you work backwards through the entire development project and how you approach it."

Sean also led a unique experience that I too got to participate in. It was a complex ecosystem that required truly understanding your customers, partners, and industry. Sean designed and led a war-gaming scenario with an outside consulting firm where we played out the role of Xbox, Sony, and Nintendo across three holiday sales periods. This became very valuable and influenced the strategy of Xbox 360. Sean told me: "We had to learn to think like Sony, with the idea that we could develop new insight into Sony's approach by playing out the likely elements of the PlayStation3 plan through 2007, and how Xbox's plan would interact with it. We looked at the console, games, services, marketing, PR, sales, distribution and then, how did Sony modify that plan based on seeing the Xbox plan in action? That was priceless because it allowed us to identify the game-changing moves, and we anticipated those successfully. We had different executives and groups role playing their counterparts at Sony, Nintendo, Xbox, and our third-party games partners. Running a real-time detailed, competitive simulation was the best way to think like Sony, to get in the Sony mind-set, including their motives and constraints. It allowed us to see how their goals were going to start changing at different points in the cycle, which ended up being very true. The importance of time played out with a simulation like that, when we saw the moves and countermoves as each company modified their plan and the market unfolded each holiday. The end result was not a precise answer predicting Sony's plans, but rather got a range of potential scenarios that prepared us for whatever moves or countermoves Sony made."

Companies such as Microsoft and Amazon have company cultures that grew and evolved over many years. The culture of a company grows a life of its own if it is not intentionally planned. Many start-up founders spend time in their initial pitches for funding defining the company they want to create. How that ideal intention plays out depends on who you hire and how strongly you uphold how you want your company to operate.

Ask yourself what legacy you want to leave. How do you want to be remembered long after you have left? What do you want your leadership legacy to be? When the media were portraying Bill Gates as pure evil during the late 1990s and the Department of Justice ruled that Microsoft had acted unfairly in the bundling of its software on hardware sales, who could have predicted that Bill Gates's legacy would not be about software, not about his aspiration in the 1980s to get a PC-on-every-desk, but philanthropy? Mark Zuckerberg credits Gates with inspiring him to make his decision on his first daughter's birth to give away 99 percent of his Facebook shares to a foundation. That multibillion-dollar decision is heavily influenced by Gates, whose legacy will transcend the software industry and Microsoft; his legacy will be teaching billionaires to influence the world through philanthropy.

While he was at Microsoft, Bill Gates inspired Microsoft employees to make charitable donations, and they have given more than $1 billion since 1981. Microsoft has an annual giving campaign in which the company matches employees' contributions as well as a Giving Day, in which employees are able to donate their time to local charities. Gates grew leaders that cared about their community and wanted to impact the world beyond their current job title.

Robbie Bach is one of those executives. He quit his 22-year career at Microsoft leading the Entertainment and Devices Division to inspire others to reengineer our communities, local governments, and nonprofit organizations. Robbie knew he was not ready to commit another five years to Microsoft, and he was ready to launch the next chapter of his life, which Robbie calls his Act II. He left Microsoft to create an army of civic engineers. Robbie has now written a book, *Xbox Revisited: A Gameplan for Corporate and Civic Renewal*, in which he shares lessons from his Microsoft years and consulting work with nonprofits and civic organizations (profits of which go to his favorite charities).

During our corporate days, Robbie was always thoughtfully ruthless with his time and protected his commitment to serve on the Boys and Girls Clubs of America board while simultaneously leading a multibillion-dollar division for Microsoft. Robbie recommends that everyone reserves one of their personal priorities for a way to impact their community. Just pick one focal point and get involved. The executives I work with who don't have any focal point outside of their job lose perspective and attach too much of their feelings of success to their current job title, salary package, and latest feedback from their boss. You can create a sense of self-worth that includes the broader impact you are having on our community.

ASSESSING YOUR CULTURE

There are six factors that define your culture, and you can plot where your company is on the cultural continuum tool in Figure 11.1. We'll return to this tool at the end of the chapter for practical ways you can use the *cultural continuum tool* in your company to accelerate your results.

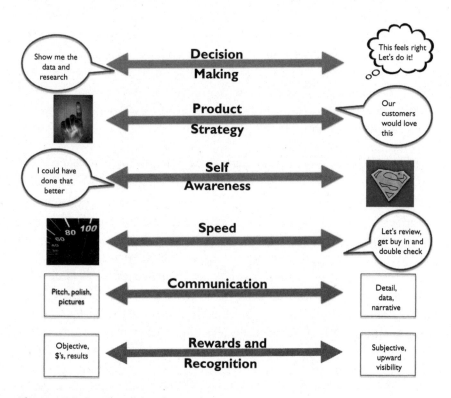

Figure 11.1   The Cultural Continuum

1. Decision Making

   Are decisions made on data, analytics, and research or based on instinct and gut reaction? You can use the decision dilemma tool in Chapter 10 to make decisions more effectively.

2. Product Strategy

   Is your product strategy driven by technology enhances and innovation or by customer obsession?

3. Self-Awareness

   How open and honest are you expected to be? Are you expected to paint a picture of a superhero and live up to that image, or are you encouraged to admit and discuss your mistakes and flaws?

4. Speed

   Which gear are you expected to be in when you are making decisions and building your business? A steady pace with a thoughtful journey mapped out or a fast trip in the express lane?

5. Communication

   Do your communications have to be pitch perfect? Is the style and delivery just as important as the content or do you have to have a maniacal attention to data, details, and specifics?

6. Rewards

   What drives your rewards and recognition? Is it pure results, objectives achieved, and numbers met? Or is it more subjective? Does managing the perception of you sideways and upwards mean greater rewards?

I developed these six cultural factors as I watched executives move between the polar opposite cultures at Microsoft and Amazon. This made transitioning executives and employees a challenge during the first three months in their role as they adapted their leadership style to the new culture they had walked into. Just like visitors to a foreign country can commit a cultural faux pas, executives can do the same when they move to a new company. You were hired for your expertise, leadership, and specific background, but now you have to operate within a new world with new rules, new rewards, and different consequences that you have been used to.

Next, we'll look at the most distinctive differences between the cultures at Amazon and Microsoft.

Pictures or a Story?

There is a company in Redmond called Silver Fox whose only job is to create PowerPoint presentations for executives, mostly from Microsoft or for businesses that are presenting to Microsoft. A whole new industry has been created to support one of Microsoft's most popular products, Power-Point. If you have never worked at a company where using Microsoft PowerPoint is the preferred method for communicating a project or a decision, or for influencing others, communicating to employees this way may seem a little farfetched. You may have to experience it to believe it. Mike Fischer, vice president of Publishing for EPIC Games, and former general manager for Marketing at Xbox said, "The presentation, in some respects, was more important than the outcome. I had two guys on my team who were just in a fighting match to see who could put the most special effects in each PowerPoint. Sometimes the animations received more applause than the business plan."

Mike also worked at Amazon, leading Digital Music in Japan, so he got to experience the Amazon narrative, where narrative documents are prepared in advance of a meeting and distributed for everyone to read, in silence. If people need more time to read, they are given it. Everyone compiles his or her thoughts and reactions, in silence. Then the meeting owner will ask for comments, page by page, on the document. This process gives everyone an equal voice and accounts for different styles of absorbing and processing information. It also prevents attendees from echoing the opinion of whoever talks the loudest, which can happen when a leader dominates a decision or debate.

When Fischer first joined in Japan, he liked the discipline of writing a six-page narrative, but it is a fine art to master: "For a new executive, it was tough to master writing a six-pager that satisfied my boss. They were just introducing more support and development as I left, but the time invest-ment inside the organization was high. It saved time for very senior executives, but the 20 revisions, reviews, and multiple meetings was not a thoughtful way to spend the team's time. One such example came when we were writing a six-pager for Amazon Instant Video, and we were deep into multiple revisions of what we would put in a direct mail campaign, agreeing on the language, the right tone, and messages when I asked, 'What about the envelope, let's discuss what is on the envelope because that is what determines if the customer will open it and read this campaign.' I was told the envelope design was decided months ago and had already gone to the printers." The cultural factors of *communication* and *decision making* play a significant part here. While the medium for making decisions can either accelerate or grind decisions to a halt, you have to make sure your team knows just when to involve the right people in crucial decisions at the right time.

Small or Large Teams?

How many people can be fed with two pizzas? That defines the size of teams at Amazon. Bezos deliberately keeps team sizes small so that innovation and new ideas can happen fast. This explains two of the cultural factors, *decision making* and *product strategy*.

Invent and Simplify

Amazon obsesses over their customers with one clear filter in mind: How can we simplify the shopping experience and how products and services are used? When Sean Gorman, COO of Panopto, was Director of the Kindle Store at Amazon, he saw a continual strong willingness to disrupt for the sake of simplicity:

I found that a lot of projects were approved on the basis of stripping out and removing complexity and making them cleaner, sometimes eliminating entire steps in the shopping experience. That kind of innovation leads to great shopping experiences. As a customer you may not even notice such changes, but you know when you shop on Amazon that it just feels effortless and delightful. That's because people approve projects to simplify and strip away complexity as opposed to adding extra buttons, extra steps, extra layers, which is a natural tendency. That cultural DNA to strive for simplification, I think was not something that I necessarily brought with me into Amazon. It was something that I learned while I was there. It was instrumental in making the Kindle Store successful.

One example is that the rights for eBooks are country specific. Publishers may own rights for certain eBooks in some countries but not others. Consequently, the eBook selection that you present to customers has to reflect what they can actually purchase in their home country. To make that work on a device often used for travel, we had to literally pivot the entire Kindle Store experience on the customer's country of origin. If we knew you were an Amazon.co.uk shopper and you lived in the UK, the selection of titles you would see and even the types of recommendations you would get, the currency, everything would be completely different than if you were some-body from the United States. We created an elegant store experience by doing a lot of real-time technical work in the background to make an informed assumption as to what country we thought you were from so you begin shopping right away. If we got it wrong, we added a little button up in the corner of the screen that would simply allow you to correct us and tell us where you were indeed from. Making that one little button pivot the entire Kindle Store in a graceful way took an extraordinary amount of work, but made it seamless for the customer.

The Very Long-Term Bet

Bezos is commonly criticized for not delivering a profit; yet, Amazon's stock price continues to grow at a phenomenal rate. The not-so-secret secret to this growth is the Amazon Flywheel that every Amazonian is taught as soon as they join the company, and Jeff Wilke recently spoke about it to the MBA class of 2017 at the University of Washington. If you offer endless selection and a remarkable experience, customers will buy, then they will return, and suppliers will want to work with you and your business will grow exponentially.

Saving Face or Admitting Your Mistakes?

The cultural factor of *self-awareness* is the most jarring unique factor of Amazon's culture. Could you imagine working in a company in which it is perfectly acceptable to admit when you make a mistake? How comfortable would you be saying in front of your peers and your boss that you made a wrong decision, or that you missed a key indicator, which cost your company millions of dollars? Could you tell others about a project your superstar team member got wrong? Would that be easy or impossible? Would you suffer retribution if you did?

Popular wisdom says you focus on your strengths, and many mistakenly interpret that to mean you hide your weaknesses and mistakes—but they are wrong. If you worked at Amazon, Jeff Bezos would not just expect that of you, he would encourage it and reward you if you demonstrate it. Not that Jeff Bezos wants you to make mistakes, but he does expect you talk about your errors, proactively share them, and learn from them.

Amazon has a crucial leadership principle called *vocally self-critical*, which Jeff Bezos personally describes like this: "Leaders do not believe that their own or their team's body odor smells of perfume." At Amazon, you are expected to come forward with problems or information, even when doing so is awkward or embarrassing.

Sean Gorman, while director of the Kindle Store, found this the most unusual aspect of Amazon's culture.

Many other companies inadvertently teach their employees that to get ahead, you need to hide your mistakes. When you show up at Amazon, you're told the opposite, which is that to succeed at Amazon you need to expose your mistakes, fix them, and prevent them from happening again. Then you need to share with everybody else so they can avoid the same mistakes. To believe this requires a leap of faith as a new employee. I began to trust that mistakes were okay when Steve Kassel, who founded the digital team at Amazon, would stand up at Amazon company-wide meetings and raise his hand to speak. He would volunteer stories about mistakes he had made, what he did to prevent them from recurring, and how he was sharing this so that other people could avoid similar mistakes. There was no need for him speak up other than to be vocally self-critical. That left a real mark on me, to the point where I was willing to do the same in my work shortly after arriving at Amazon. Whenever I made a mistake, instead of sweeping it under the rug, I immediately raised alarm bells and told everybody it. I then briefed a wide audience, summarizing, "Here's the scope of the problem. Here's what went wrong. Here's how we could have learned faster from our mistake and reacted faster. Here's how we have prevented recurrence. And here's how we're sharing and documenting it so others will avoid this same mistake." This was very helpful in creating an environment in my organization where people weren't afraid to experiment. They were willing to try new things and take risks, especially if these were two-way doors, meaning that the decisions and actions were reversible, as opposed to one-way doors where you can't go back. I carried this mind-set with me beyond Amazon. At every Panopto all-hands meeting, I am the one who stands up to tell the entire company about some new mistake I made, what I did to fix it and prevent it from happening again, and how I hope other people can learn from it.

If this is one of your aspirational cultural moves, here are four fast ways you can help your company become more vocally self-critical:

1. Start with you.

    You have to be a role model. Start sharing what you would have done differently so others do the same. In my first week at Amazon, I was in a meeting with two vice presidents and a handful of others. We were reviewing the progress of a strategic project. One vice president said, "I could have done a better job putting more resources on this project in the last few months. I will fix that now." The other replied, "Great, and I wasn't close enough to the details to make sure this was on track to meet the deadline. I am now." That level of honesty in some companies would be a severe career-limiting move, but at Amazon it is encouraged.

2. Hire for brutal honesty.

Don't ask the futile interview question, "What are your weaknesses?" Instead, ask candidates to tell you about a time they made a mistake. Listen and probe for how they tell the story. Do they acknowledge how they contributed to the mistake, or do they blame everyone around them? Are they comfortable telling the story or do you have to drag it out of them? This will tell you if they can work in an organization where self-reflection and vulnerability is the norm.

3. Make it a condition for success.

At Amazon before you promote someone, you have to identify the "best reason not to promote them" (which has to be a real reason, not something fake like they work too hard). This identifies whether their manager has a blind spot for them or if they can see where they need to complement their strengths with other people or take corrective action.

4. Get others' input.

Jeff Bezos insists that every leader gets feedback once a year. This includes how they embody the Amazon leadership principles. This isn't some arbitrary rating or score but evidence-based feedback and examples that impact how people are rewarded and inform their development conversations with their manager.

It may take some time to get used to this, but every Amazonian I have met who has left Amazon said it was the most career-enhancing part of their Amazon experience. Although it required backbone, they said it gave them the freedom and safety to tell the whole truth and nothing but the truth.

Customer or Employee Obsessed?

Amazon's customer obsession is commendable. It is the pivotal reason they can create so much innovation rapidly, and their marketing and communication to customers is refreshing and inspiring. To continue to grow, Amazon is going to need to apply this equally to their employees.

Innovation occurs when candid conversations happen at every level of the organization. Microsoft needs to shift its pendulum away from employees and closer to its customers, which Satya Nadella is reported to be doing.

CAN YOU TAKE THE HEAT?

The true test of how thoughtfully ruthless a leader is occurs when he is acting under pressure. Now with our always-on and always-sharing culture, it takes seconds for your actions or statements to be broadcast to the world. Acting under intense scrutiny and criticism requires a calm and poise that tests many leaders' resolve. Steve Ballmer worked for several years under media calls for his resignation; yet, he calmly went about his business, not addressing it directly and trying to be judged by his bold actions of acquiring Nokia, reorganizing the company, and continuing to profess his belief in Microsoft's mobile strategy.

Jeff Bezos takes a more direct approach to criticism. When the book *The Amazon Store* was published, Bezos did not like what he read. The irony that Bezos was selling and profiting from a book that was critical of his leadership style and decisions was not lost on many inside and outside of Amazon. It was almost comical that his wife, Mackensie, would write a lengthy one-star review disputing many of the facts and representations of Bezos and Amazon's early years. Several other members of Amazon's executive team also posted one-star reviews disputing the credibility and facts of the book. In the words of Macbeth, maybe he "doth protest too much."

Bezos recently hired a former press secretary to the president to lead his public affairs, which may explain the increase in the public battles Bezos has been recently willing to fight. When the *New York Times* ran the "Inside Amazon: Wrestling Big Ideas in a Bruising Workplace" story in the summer of 2015 every CEO, leadership expert, and financial investor were dissecting every aspect of that brutal storytelling. I wasn't surprised that a journalist could find 100 disgruntled employees from a company that employs 180,000. What was surprising was Bezos's reaction, after a perfectly reasonable rebuttal post, he then went after one individual and discredited him personally and professionally. While those facts may have been true, to put a spotlight on one individual in a report that covered many aspects of Amazon's culture seemed one step too far on the ruthlessness scale.

The *New York Times* article defined Amazon's perception in the job marketplace. You don't have to spend much time in a downtown coffee shop in Seattle, home to Amazon's headquarters, to overhear a recruiter or a manager hiring for their team and discussing what it is like to work at Amazon. Conventional wisdom may say this will hurt Amazon's ability to continue its hiring ramp, but I disagree. It will actually help them.

Amazon has a unique culture, one that may not suit everyone. Armchair corporate commentary is easy and often misguided. Until you live, breathe, and become an Amazonian, as I did on the fashion leadership team during explosive growth, it is impossible to understand. Imagine having a job where your sole purpose is to delight customers and where you are free to challenge your boss and your boss's boss as long as you back up your arguments with data. Wouldn't you want to work at a place where all of your time, energy, and resources are spent obsessing over customers, rather than internal drama? Prove you have an innovative idea, as I did, and you will get fast funding and approval to go hire a team to create your dream idea.

Ambitious, determined, focused entrepreneurs don't choose a career in civil service at a local government office.

Similarly, anyone looking for two-hour lunch breaks and an easy workload shouldn't choose to work in a fast-growing Fortune 500 company that sprouts more innovation every 12 months than many companies create in a lifetime. Amazonians who did their research well prior to accepting a job offer should not be surprised. When I read the *New York Times* article, I winced at some of the personal examples, but quietly nodded along with some of the points concerning intense focus and relentlessness.

Amazon is experiencing what is becoming the new corporate flagrant weakness: investing in too much talent. They are trying to hire too fast. Like many CEOs of fast-growing companies, Bezos targeted top industry talent to run new initiatives in TV, fashion, cloud services, drones, and gaming. New executives arrive, and they are expected to *drive for results* and have a *bias for action* (referring to two of the 14 Amazon leadership principles); yet, they don't have the right teams in place to go and execute on all of the great ideas.

This has created many tornados inside their rapidly growing divisions because initiatives are not scaled back or prioritized when the team is only

50 percent staffed. The team just has to absorb the extra work. If you are in a team that is staffed fully, your experience is remarkably more positive.

REWARD THE RESULTS YOU WANT

Ballmer didn't always get his communication right. In 2013, when he announced the company's largest restructuring in its history, he used a 2,763-word e-mail to explain the new company divisions. This, just three months prior to his resignation, could have been his defining moment for inspiring the then 90,000 employees behind his new vision. He was breaking down the silos and the divisions and attempting to create One-Microsoft that innovated and collaborated, except he left out the one vital key that would unlock the success: changing how people are rewarded. In the already highly competitive company, individual perform-ance is rewarded. There were rarely team goals, and team or divisional rewards did not exist. If Ballmer truly wanted to transform the company, he needed to change the rewards to put bite into the cultural fluffy words of *One-Microsoft*. The reality is that if it doesn't show in your pay packet, you are going to manage to what you are rewarded for. What Ballmer should have said in a much briefer company e-mail is:

> Dear Microsoft,
>
> I recognize this is an about-turn for how we have operated in the past. Say good-bye to our business unit silos; we are arranging by function and now need to work horizontally to better serve our customers. To make sure we succeed, I am realigning everyone's compensation to support the collaboration required. Annual bonuses and stock awards will now be linked to team and company goals, so we can put Company, Team, and Individual needs in that order.
>
> Steve Ballmer

In contrast, Amazon's culture has teeth. New hires are interviewed against the Amazon leadership principles. Everyone gets spontaneous feedback twice a year against how well you are demonstrating the leader-ship principles. To get promoted, your manager has to provide written examples of how you demonstrate the leadership principles. If you are getting promoted to a management role or into a director or VP role, you have to have significant strength in *hire and develop the best*. So people leaders have to actually demonstrate great people leadership, which is an oxymoron in many companies.

UNLEASHING INNOVATION

You can raise $10 million on Kickstarter in a month. The idea that you had on the back of a notebook for five years can either be thrown out or be validated with funding in 30 days. The speed from idea to execution has recently exploded. No longer do you have to wait years to tinker with your idea and figure out how to get funding. Kickstarter alone has helped more than 94,000 companies raise more than $2 billion of funding, and large corporations such as Amazon and Microsoft have to find new unique ways to tap into the innovation itches of its employees so they don't experience innovation-brain-drain. They need to unleash the innovative ideas and passions of their employees internally so they don't quit and go test their idea out on Kickstarter.

Amazon has started to do this with its new businesses whether it is fashion, drone technology, self-publishing books, t-shirt creation, or tapping its 472 million customers to become Uber-style delivery drivers. They are breaking the mold on innovation.

First, Bezos knows he has to go after magnet hires in the industry he wants to disrupt. He hired Cathy Beaudoin from Gap when Amazon wanted to launch Amazon's new fashion business. More recently, he hired British car journalist Jeremy Clarkson, who built his success on crazy car stunts on *Top Gear* that used to gain an estimated worldwide audience of 350 million viewers. He is often in the news for all of the wrong reasons. Most recently, he was publicly fired by the BBC for physically attacking a member of his production team. But that didn't stop Bezos from paying $250 million for three seasons of shows with Clarkson and his two co-presenters Richard Hammond and James May. Bezos knows he has to target global household names such as Clarkson to boost their ratings of original content on Amazon Prime as they continue to chase Netflix in the video-streaming space.

Amazon will often conduct small, fast experiments across different small teams to rapidly innovate. One example, which could be gearing up for drone-ready tracking, is Prime Now, which launched in Los Angeles last month. I have been delighted to benefit from this new service where I can order groceries and gifts and get them delivered for free in less than two hours. This service competes with its existing Amazon Fresh grocery delivery service. For some companies, this would have caused the concept to come to a grinding halt, but not at Amazon. Fast experimentation and rapid sun-setting of projects that don't work provide insights from customers in less time than it takes some companies to still be planning a launch.

Amazon Prime Now lets you track on a map exactly where your delivery driver is and how long before your parcel arrives at your doorstep. This is just the technology that could be used for tracking your drone as it flies across freeways and fields to your house.

USING THE CULTURAL CONTINUUM

There are many practical ways you can use the cultural continuum tool. First, you can use it to define your current culture, and you may then want to use it to define your future culture. What elements do you want to leave behind and which ones do you want to change? When you see the delta, you can then develop a plan for making that cultural change.

You can also use the cultural continuum tool to help explain your culture to those who are interviewing to join your company. By using behavioral interviewing questions to understand the interviewee's preferences and approaches, you can assess if they would be a good fit for your company. For example, you could ask: "Tell me about a time you recently made a significant decision. How did you reach your decision?" By asking additional probing questions to their example, you can identify how their current company operates and what their own personal preferred approach is. You need to be brutally honest about how your company operates when hiring, otherwise you create turmoil on the new employee roller coaster when they join you.

After using it to help with hiring, you can then use it to help launch new leaders and employees in your company so that you can reduce the time it takes them to reach full productivity in their role. Understanding and adapting to the culture takes more time and energy than any technical or knowledge-based challenge. This will help avoid haphazard understanding, which is happening at Amazon as their average length of service is reported to be just 12 months. There are more new leaders than old leaders everywhere, and they're all trying to figure out a peculiar culture that creates rapid innovation but is hard to understand. Don't let your new leaders learn your culture in a haphazard way. Ruthlessly prioritize, giving them the support they need to understand how your company works and apply that knowledge. Provide coaching and mentoring as they make the cultural leap from their last company to yours. Beyond new employees, this can also be used to give feedback to others on how they are acting within the culture. You can define where there are strengths and gaps against each of the six cultural factors.

THE EXPRESS LANE TO CULTURE CHANGE

Most change efforts fail, especially when the goal is to make significant cultural changes. In a quarter of a century of leading successful and failed change efforts, I have seen one sure-fire, guaranteed way to change culture fast: change the leader at the top.

At Microsoft, Satya Nadella is proving this theory to be correct. Already he has canceled those cringeworthy rah-rah company meetings. Now he has a hacker day in which the whole company participates in innovation challenges. He is encouraging a growth mind-set and attempting to get groups to collaborate more. But if there is no bite with rewards, it will be a long and painful road to significant changes that matter to stockholders and customers. Time will tell.

Chapter 12

MIND THE GAP

This chapter explains how you can take immediate action today and create an early warning system to ensure your good intentions don't fall through the gap. It covers the common excuses leaders give for not being thoughtfully ruthless, how to overcome them, and how to course-correct along the way so you have the unlimited energy, increased discretionary time, and remarkable team to support you as a thoughtfully ruthless leader. Finally, it prepares you for the success you are about to experience as well as how to handle yourself when you have additional time, energy, and resources at your disposal.

EVAPORATING EXCUSES

As this book comes to its conclusion, I realize I could spend an entire chapter talking about excuses, but that would excuse me from actually wrapping up this book with powerful, meaningful insights that will inspire you to go from simply thinking to actually taking action about becoming more thoughtfully ruthless. This is the precise point in reading a book where excuses pop up like bamboo shoots bursting through the ground, eager to grab anything nearby and choke the life out of it. If you have taken action prior to reading this chapter, you are already ahead of the curve. "Anything you can do, I can do better, I can do anything better than you. NO YOU CAN'T, YES I CAN, NO YOU CANT, YES I CAN, NO YOU CANT, YES I CAN, YES I CAN, YES I CAN!"

This song from the Broadway show *Annie Get Your Gun* says it all, endless arguing about who does it better. Rather than spending time thinking and debating doing something, or a better way to do something, actually go and do something! In Seattle, traffic congestion is out of control. For 20 years, city officials have been arguing about whether to build a bridge, a mass transit system, or a tunnel connecting across Lake Washington. In that time, traffic has increased a thousandfold, and by the time the bridge is complete in 2016, it will likely be inadequate for the volume of current vehicles. If only they had made a decision 20 years ago; imagine all the time and money that would have been saved!

I have watched leaders pontificate in all kinds of businesses about what to do first for so long that by the time they make their decision, everything has changed. Speed is of the essence to the thoughtfully ruthless leader.

There are likely many excuses sprouting in your head right now about why it is hard to be thoughtfully ruthless. Here are the top three reasons that I hear:

1. I don't want to appear aloof. I want to show that I can roll up my sleeves and do the work as well as lead.

   Retort: Just stop that; your job now is to focus on looking up and looking out and creating followership with your team. Focus on the right spot.

2. I am working on managing my time, which should get me close to where I want to go.

   Retort: You are not the Energizer bunny banging on the toy drum. Unless you also focus on your own energy reserves, you cannot plow through and go on forever. Focus on your resources available to you and how you can recharge your own batteries.

3. I hate the word *ruthless*, it has such negative connotations. I am not a brutal leader.

   Retort: That is why you have to be thoughtful about where you are ruthless. Many leaders who don't like the concept of being too ruthless often excessively worry about how much they are liked. Instead, consider how you can be respected and thoughtful about when you need to be more intentional and deliberate.

Mind the Gap is the warning on the London Underground as you leave the train and step on the platform. In reality it is just a 10-inch gap, but still the health and safety obsessives feel it necessary to paint giant signs reminding the British public to mind-the-gap as though it will be a surprise to them. It's so obvious that the gap is there! But what is not quite so obvious is the gap that exists in many executives' heads when they consider where their business or team is today and where they want it to go in the future. That future opportunity gap (FOG) has a foggy acronym for a reason. You need to figure out how you will battle the FOG, which is where out-standing leaders differentiate themselves from the rest. Some find it hard to see through the fog, others cut straight through.

Consider your own FOG. Where is your greatest gap that would give you the most return on effort? Is it becoming more thoughtfully ruthless with your energy, your resources, or your time—or perhaps even a combination? Consider the gap that exists between where you are today, how you used to work, and your future goals. Deliberately decide what you will focus on.

Here are the four priority zones to focus on:
1. Name one of your strengths, that you could role model for others in your company.
2. Pick one priority area for you to personally change.
3. Identify one area your team needs to collectively work on.
4. Pick an area you want your boss or your board of directors to focus on.

Now you have your *four priority zones*, you have to be prepared for course corrections along the way, which is where you will see some of your most rapid results.

PREPARE FOR ABRUPT U-TURNS

One of my executive clients seemed to be failing to make progress against his goals. I couldn't quite understand why. I knew he knew what to do, but he would regularly miss our agreed upon deadlines. In one of our conversations, I asked him one simple question: "What is really going on? You repeatedly miss deadlines and I feel like a broken record. You aren't getting the value you could be out of our work together."

That started a frank and transparent conversation that he felt we were moving too fast. He felt he couldn't really talk about his real struggles with what he was trying to achieve because he knew we kept talking about the same topics, but he wasn't making the progress we were supposed to be. We immediately took a U-turn in our work together. I realized my pace was too fast, and I needed to spend more time building understanding of what we were working on and why. We talked about how he needed to tell me to slow down and to tell me if he didn't understand so we could start there more often. This completely changed how we worked together. Now, several months later, he is having more success and rapidly achieving his goals. Most important, our conversations are transparent and provocative. Being prepared for U-turns and having honest dramatic dialogue with advisors you trust will accelerate your goals to becoming thoughtfully ruthless.

CHANGE YOUR VIEW, CHANGE YOUR HABITS

Visual stimulation is the most critical success factor in changing habits. Think about this:

- If you see a cookie, you are more likely to start thinking about wanting to eat one.
- If you walk past a fabulous looking cocktail bar, you are more likely to start thinking about your favorite drink or hanging out with friends.
- If you see the e-mail notification on your laptop, you are more likely to go and check your in-box.
- If you see your phone on the kitchen counter, you are more likely to pick it up and check any number of messaging apps or social media.
- If you see a welcome friend down the street, you are more likely to go and say hello.
- If you have a picture of your favorite holiday destination on your office wall, you are likely to remember memories from your last trip.
- If you have your daily goals written on a piece of paper on your desk, you are more likely to focus on achieving them.

Creating visual triggers will help you reinforce good habits and eliminate habits you want to replace. Take a tour of your house or office and make note of what is a distraction and what is a positive reinforcement of your goals.

I write faster and more efficiently when I am not in my office or I am in different surroundings. Huntington Library or a local coffee shop with outside seating are my favorite writing spots or at the bottom of my garden, underneath my palm tree, away from distracting Wi-Fi. I also leave my phone on my desk in my home office at the end of my day, not checking it again until the next morning. I also leave it on the other side of my office when I am working rather than in reach. As a result, I can focus faster when I am writing, and I am reading more each evening. I also have a deliberate start to my day because my traditional alarm clock is waking me. That way I am not in my in-box or checking news sites within 60 seconds of my brain waking.

LISTEN TO WHO YOU LISTEN TO

There is free advice everywhere for you to seek out or where others seek you out to give spontaneous unrequested feedback. Some companies endlessly survey their employees and even link their employees' happiness to executives' pay, which is the most ridiculously divisive possible approach. Thoughtfully ruthless leaders won't always make their teams happy—that is what clowns, comedy shows, and bad jokes are for. Your role as a thoughtfully ruthless leader is to grow your business, grow your value for your investors, and grow your employees. Your role is to be respected, not liked. You want to earn followers, not friends. You want to be sought out for your insights, not your affection. Don't get distracted by ridiculous incentives that misguided human resources people have put in place.

EVIDENCE, PATTERNS, AND OBSERVED BEHAVIOR

Leadership development is a $5 billion dollar industry that fails to produce quantifiable results. The biggest reason is there are human resources professionals inside organizations as well as many external experts suggesting that retreats, team building, and training will improve leaders' lives without any connection to how your business will improve as a result. Don't waste time on assessments, team building, and personal development that puts a label on your head about the type of leader/communicator/decision maker that you are. Such endeavors have as much impact on business results as the latest quiz overtaking Facebook feeds everywhere: "Which Star Wars character are you?"

An executive I know was recently told by an executive coach that she is a "D" leader and militaristic in her leadership style. She told me the whole time with her executive coach was spent talking about her label and what it meant. Not once did she and the coach discuss her business goals, aspirations, or the adaptations that could be made to accelerate her strategic plan or growth as a leader. What a missed opportunity. Don't waste your valuable time; instead, follow these five steps to become a thoughtfully ruthless leader:

1. Know your destination.

    Set clear goals for where you want to grow and improve. Not everyone wants to become the CEO. It is okay if your goal is to get back to doing what you love, whether that is designing products, writing code, or leading a small team. Give your team permission to tell you their true aspirations and ask: What goal are you aiming for?

2. Get specific feedback from people you trust.

    Unsolicited feedback (which is often given without your best interests at heart) can knock you off course and distract you. Consider whose feedback you trust, and ask if they would be willing to provide you with feedback over the next six months on the specific areas you are working on. I was working with a CEO who followed this advice as he was working on improving how he focused on the future growth of his business; he approached one member of his team and two of his board members and asked them to let him know if he was focusing too much on short-term tactics rather than on long-term business growth. They acted as his guardrail to keep him on track. Who could you ask to do the same for you?

3. Identify your accelerators and decelerators.

    Do you know what knocks you off course and distracts you? Write that list now. Then write a list of everything that accelerates your performance—what situations, which people, and what has to be happening for you to be at your peak. For me, I have to be regularly exercising. If I have skipped CrossFit for a week, I find I am lethargic and can't focus as well. What are your accelerators, and how can you develop a plan to remove your decelerators and maintain your accelerators for peak performance?

4. Galvanize your team around your goals.

    The fastest way to improve your leadership ability is to have a strong team around you. Know where your business will be in two years, hire forward, and get that team in place now. Then make sure your team is aligned with clear goals and expectations. Where do you need to act to galvanize your team?

5. Create dramatic dialogue.

Successful leaders create dramatic dialogue. Disruptive disagreement is healthy, and challenging conversations will help you and your business grow faster. Do you shy away from conversations that could be difficult or do you ask provocative questions, allow people to disagree with you, and encourage direct honest conversations? What new conversations do you need to start today?

The most successful entrepreneurs have strong mentors and coaches. Just like elite athletes, they know that to improve their performance they need immediate feedback and encouragement in the right places. Be wary if you are asked to use dubious assessments to reveal if you are a purple squirrel or a green giraffe. Instead, insist on creating meaningful results that impact profit, revenue, and personal success.

PRACTICE ALTITUDE ADJUSTMENT

Gregg Glassman started as a personal trainer at Gold's Gym and built the multimillion-dollar business of CrossFit Inc., which created the billion-dollar industry of affiliates, equipment, nutrition, and apparel. When I met Greg Glassman after he spoke at the University of Washington several years ago I asked him what he saw as the greatest differentiation factor that either catapulted or slowed down company and executive growth.

"How you adjust your altitude," he replied. "It's like being in a rocket ship where you have to adjust from operating it at 5,000, 10,000, and 15,000 feet." Glassman and I agree that only a select number of leaders can make that altitude change and succeed on their own. Others need some help and can get there, and for the final group, their sweet spot may be at a smaller size and scale. Knowing where your sweet spot is and knowing even when to fire yourself as the CEO or leader of a growing business is what will define you as a thoughtfully ruthless leader.

MAKE UNPOPULAR AND HIGH-RISK DECISIONS

To prepare for your success, sometimes you have to be ruthless and take a thoughtful bet on one of your team. When Andrea Leigh, general manager of Amazon's Canada business, was launching the fashion site in Canada, her team had aggressive goals. Andrea gave her team this challenge: How can we set up the most vendors on our site in the shortest possible time so that on launch day customers see the most brands possible available for purchase? She knew automation was the key but needed to find someone who rapidly had the capability and capacity to make it happen.

"Technical talent was a hot commodity at Amazon, so I needed someone on my current team who could automate the vendor set up process. I found someone who had a basic understanding, but more importantly he had the one crucial trait: intellectual curiosity. So I gave him the challenge and gave him permission to make this his number one priority, even if it meant ignoring some of his day job and frankly, annoying the rest of his team mates because he was solely focused on this one priority." Launch day came and over a million items were on the Canadian site for Amazon and it was heralded a success. "It wasn't a popular decision at the time, but the customer benefited and so did our business. I knew I had to find the right talent, ruthlessly prioritize, and find out what was important to him so he could be appropriately rewarded if we achieved joint success," said Andrea.

Accountability Forces Habits

If you don't achieve one of your goals and no one knew about it, does anyone care? You always have a choice about how you share your goals:

- Option A: Declaring to yourself will improve the probability of your success, a little.
- Option B: Declaring to others your intentions and goals will improve your probability of success remarkably.
- Option C: Declaring to others and asking for their help holding you accountable will dramatically improve the likelihood of your success.

Option C is the fastest path to success, which requires vulnerability and confidence.

When I decided to start yoga, I shared my commitment with a few people who matter: my chiropractor, my CrossFit coaches, and a couple of yoga-loving friends. I asked them to ask me every time they saw me how many times I had practiced yoga that week. Knowing they would be interested improved the probability I would practice. Consider what you are working on improving right now—who could you share it with to gain encouragement and support?

Using Your Excess Time, Energy, and Resources

What would you do if you won the lottery may be a question that you ask close friends over a long dinner, but it is a valid question to ask as you consider your intentional wishful thinking.

- If your goal is to take more vacation, where will you travel?
- If your goal is to earn a million dollars, what will your life be like when you have that income?
- If you goal is to retire, how do you plan to spend the next chapter of your life?
- If your goal is to work less, what will you do with your time each day, week, and month?

Making a plan for how you will make the most of your success will paint a picture of perfection that will inspire you and help you see what is possible.

Ten Thoughtfully Ruthless Success Principles

Finally if you follow these 10 thoughtfully ruthless success principles, you will accelerate toward becoming the leader you want to be:

1. Know your next ultimate goal and filter ruthlessly to achieve it.
   Don't spend too long considering what your goal could possibly be; pick one and move forward.
2. Make sure your doing is outweighing your thinking.
   Switch off your overthinking and pre-worry, move fast to action, and course correct along the way. Hours spent planning could be hours doing and seeing results.
3. Pick a priority one at a time.
   Know your immediate priority and filter your calendar, your inbox, and your mental capacity around that one priority. When it is complete, pick and move onto the next.
4. Throw out at least 20 percent of your calendar each week.
   Priorities rapidly change; yet, calendars sometimes appear chiseled in stone. Review your current priorities and lose 20 percent of your commitments and meetings by canceling, declining your participation, or giving it to a member of your team.

5. Train like a marathon.

    Know what it will take to run your 26-mile equivalent, pace yourself, and set up appropriate rewards along the way.

6. Fast upgrade your team.

    You likely have one person in mind right now who would be better suited in a different role on a different team or in a different company. Make a fast decision and act, then move onto your next work-in-progress leader until you have the team that can carry your business through to the size and scale you will be in five years time.

7. Delegate away your day job.

    Imagine you were going on a three-month extended vacation. Who could you delegate which parts of your job to? Now reconsider who could take parts of your job right now that would stretch and grow them and give you the capacity to take on more strategic work.

8. Create your own thoughtfully ruthless community.

    Who is in your inner circle today that you would like to keep there? Who are the targets that you would like to add? Now build a regular connection for them where you see them either individually or collectively and talk about how you are becoming more thoughtfully ruthless and how you can help each other. Start thoughtfully ruthless circles where you share how thoughtfully ruthless you are with your time, energy, and resources and where you need advice and ideas.

9. Make the first 15 and last 15 minutes of your day count.

    Intentionally use the first 15 and last 15 minutes of your day to set your goals, reprioritize your calendar, and then review your accomplishments to gather insights and plan your next day.

10. Surround yourself with people who energize and inspire you.

    Identify the most inspirational people you know and spend more time with them, and target new people you want to include in your inner circle. Start divorce proceedings from those colleagues and friends who aren't supporting, pushing, and inspiring you. Prioritize people who make you laugh until you cry in your life.

By now you will have seen how you can grow your business faster and have more time to use as you choose—all while becoming more energized and inspired. You will be promoted faster than your peers. You will be head hunted by more companies to join them. You will have more time to use as you choose. You will become more energized and inspired. By becoming a thoughtfully ruthless leader, your heart will feel full because your focus is on people and work that you love.

Champion race horses wear blinders while they race because they prevent the horses from getting distracted. I'd encourage you to be thoughtfully ruthless with your blinders so that you are focused on the results you want and you can be first across the finish line.

Yours, ruthlessly thoughtful.

APPENDIX

A dynamic online version of the appendix is available at www .valwrightconsulting.com/thoughtfullyruthless including bonus updated content.

NINETY-NINE WAYS TO BE THOUGHTFULLY RUTHLESS WITH YOUR TIME

1. Wear earphones so people who you don't want to talk to you, won't.
2. Stop activities, projects, and responsibilities faster than you start them.
3. Spend 50 percent of your time with your new hires in their first month.
4. Spend 10 percent of your time with the rising stars in your organization.
5. Intentionally dedicate time to your two- to three-year business focus.
6. Unfairly allocate your time, biasing toward your highest-performing individuals.
7. Rapidly tackle underperformance or mismatched employees; don't delay and don't overthink.
8. Schedule your to-do list into your calendar.
9. Plan your year every December: book holidays, experiences, family time, friends' time, couple time, and me time.
10. Find your PPP, your perfect productive places, where you are your most productive.
11. Become a squatter in different offices, buildings, coffee shops, or libraries to escape interruptions.
12. Only allow customers, clients, potential buyers, and your employees into your in-box. Auto-sort everything else into folders.

13. Start your day by writing down your goals for the day; place it visibly on your desk.
14. Let your team know your love/hate list for e-mail, phone calls, meetings, and messaging.
15. Do the "don't want to but need to" items at the start of every day.
16. Turn off the e-mail auto-send to your phone.
17. Shut down outlook, reminders, pop-ups, and notifications.
18. Use a paper calendar on your wall.
19. Only communicate what is necessary—cut out the intro, the justification, and the recap.
20. Start every e-mail with "My question is . . . ," "I need . . . ," "Will you please . . ."
21. Schedule tasks in your calendar as soon as you receive them.
22. Shut down your calendar, in-box, and documents an hour before the end of your day.
23. Spend the last hour of your day on "your choice" activities, not urgent outstanding work.
24. Schedule time to evaluate all of your meetings every two months. Dump those that don't add value.
25. Teach your team and peers how to interact with you and reciprocate.
26. Use a presumptive close such as "Let's meet at 12 noon on Thursday" rather than "What time works for you?"
27. Hold 15-, 30-, or 45-minute meetings.
28. End meetings at random times if you have achieved the goals.
29. End meetings 10 minutes early. Use the time to complete actions fast.
30. Start your day with the big projects, not the sweep-the-floor tasks (picking up e-mail, following up).
31. Use your time calculator on tasks, meetings, and projects. Check to make sure (return on effort).
32. Calculate the cost of your most difficult client or employee. Is it good investment for your focus?
33. Schedule in everything: your blog writing, customer visits, and open space think time.
34. Weekend and evening e-mail is selfish. Save it in your drafts and send in regular business hours or auto-schedule it for sensible hours.

35. Out of hours e-mail generates out of hours e-mail. You will get a response that you feel obliged to respond to and you will develop expectations that you are always on and available.
36. Don't follow technology fads if they suck up your team's time. Slack, Skype, Zoom, FaceTime should be introduced only if they improve and remove other communications, not add to it.
37. Set your daily, weekly, monthly, and quarterly tasks and book them into your calendar.
38. Know your procrastination destination so you can create barriers to getting there.
39. Never go to sleep with an outstanding invoice to send.
40. Powerful words: of course.
41. Add a day onto your work trip so you fly back the morning after the last day of a learning event. Take time to relax, to reflect, and to plan your implementation.
42. Dine alone once a month.
43. Use a car service to make time to think, breathe, make calls, or decompress during drive time.
44. Create two-way door decisions—ones that can be reversed—for speedier decisions.
45. Create your just-stop-it guide and have it visible daily.
46. Correlate the time it takes to buy something with the actual value. Don't spend an hour deciding which $30 gadget to choose—decide and move.
47. Create rituals for the beginning and end of day to focus on your goals and achievements.
48. Know your preferred approach to deadlines and adapt to deliver early.
49. Block multiple silence-slots into your calendar for thinking and ideation.
50. Improve your thought: action ratio; get faster at doing, not thinking.
51. Develop a robust employee launch plan for new members of your team.
52. Know when to say no, without justification or overthinking.
53. Dust off your camera and use it to take pictures; keep your phone in your pocket where it won't distract you.
54. Bring back your old alarm clock; leave your phone downstairs, not by your bed.

55. Use your watch to tell the time rather than your phone, which will suck you into checking messages.
56. Simplify your life: ask what is taking up your time that you can get rid of.
57. Auto-pilot your social life with first Monday of the month dinners and Friday lunch dates. Simplify logistics and eliminate endless scheduling e-mails.
58. Regularly reevaluate your whole life. What are your goals for two years time? How can you get there faster?
59. Slow down to speed up; everything doesn't have to happen at 90 m.p.h.
60. Ten minutes a day is better than procrastinating for a month. Break daunting goals into small chunks.
61. Start tasks at the earliest possible opportunity, not at the last available opportunity.
62. If you have a pattern of missing deadlines, understand the root cause and fix it.
63. If you regularly leave deadlines until the last possible time, find an accountability partner to help you deliver early.
64. Reset your deadline demands with your team so they know what is acceptable.
65. If you regularly allow others to cancel and reschedule last minute, you are enabling them to disrespect your time. Reset what is acceptable.
66. Cut the small talk and get to the point.
67. Spend 25 percent of your team meetings talking about people and leadership topics.
68. Switch your phone and laptop into offline mode for uninterrupted work time.
69. Don't open your e-mail unless you are going to respond.
70. If you have openings on your immediate team, spend 50 percent of your time hiring, interviewing, and asking for referrals.
71. Create clear instructions for how you want people to interact with you: Can they disagree in public? Do you want data-backed discussions? Tell them your preferences so they are not guessing.
72. Don't use ego-invites in meetings; invite people who will contribute.
73. Pay attention to your meeting room furniture—is it alienating or including everyone in attendance?
74. Block time off to leave your desk and go for a walk each day.

75. Create an end-of-day ritual where you tidy your desk, organize your network and physical work, and plan tomorrow.

76. Create an end-of-week ritual where you review your successes, reflect on your insights, and plan for next week.

77. Set celebrations for when you have achieved key milestones.

78. Use your calendar to commit to frequent exercise.

79. Set your alarm clock for 30 minutes earlier Monday through Friday, and use the extra 2.5 hours for yourself.

80. Don't waste time on TV shows or movies you don't enjoy; read a book or go to sleep.

81. Perform a weekly check: make sure you are getting enough discretionary time to use as you choose.

82. Rate every one of your meetings: exemplary, could do better, energy zapper. Change the latter two.

83. Tear up your to-do list: create a to-don't list of activities that are not worth your time.

84. Don't create a to-do list; create specific time blocks in your calendar and assign tasks to that time.

85. Deliberately assign time to managing upward with your boss.

86. Systematically allocate time to building relationships with your peers.

87. Intentionally build relationships and seek advice from your board members and investors.

88. Go visit customers—hear directly how they use your products and services.

89. Play "back-to-the-floor" once a year; go and answer phones in customer service, work directly in the test team, and get on the front lines.

90. Intentionally balance time away from activities and actions that sit in the next 30-day window—look up and look out.

91. Complete a calendar review every two months to check that your recurring meetings haven't grown a life of their own.

92. Don't spin in the regret-roulette wheel; if you need to look backward, use fast reflection to gain immediate insights and decide what action you will take.

93. Don't use a paragraph when a sentence will do, don't use a sentence when a word will do, and don't use a word when silence will do.

94. Cut your preparation in half and experiment with the results.

95. Help others get to the point faster: Ask, "What do you need?"
96. Every phone call cuts out at least 10 e-mails.
97. Listen more than you talk, you will learn more.
98. Act based on evidence, patterns, and themes.
99. Be okay with messy—not everything has to be perfect, pretty, and perfectly poised.

NINETY-NINE WAYS TO BE THOUGHTFULLY RUTHLESS WITH YOUR ENERGY

1. Laugh at yourself, don't take yourself so seriously, let your team know your strengths, your flaws, and what you want from them, laughter.
2. Have at least three people on speed dial that you can call for candid advice—people who have your best interests at heart.
3. Identify your accelerators and decelerators to being inspired and energized.
4. Always have a coach who is working with you to accelerate your goals.
5. Take the seven-day sleep test: try getting an additional hour's sleep each night, repeat seven nights, and check how you feel.
6. Identify and build relationships with aspirational peers.
7. Create your perfect nutrition rules and follow them 80 percent of the time.
8. Create your perfect exercise plan rules and follow them 80 percent of the time.
9. Stop the worry trifecta of pre-worry, parallel worry, and post-worry.
10. Create an enviable inner circle of advisors.
11. Start saying no to people who don't energize and inspire you.
12. Turn on your drama-detector: avoid people and situations who attract drama.
13. Spend zero energy on conclusions that cannot be changed.
14. Stop yourself from spinning the regret-roulette wheel if you cannot change the outcome.
15. Create intentional habits you are going to break and re-create.
16. Check if you are at the point of debate or point of conclusion so you know where to expend your energy.
17. Know your energy leaks and plug the holes.

18. Surround yourself with people who believe in you.

19. Become imperturbable and don't let little things knock you off course.

20. Allow others to return your serve; don't act like an automatic tennis ball dispenser firing ideas, instructions, and challenges in every direction at lightning speed.

21. Great nutrition is an investment; invest in yourself and find what works for you for right now.

22. Find exercise that you love and feels fun—protect it on your calendar ruthlessly.

23. Focus your team's time on customers, products, and profit—not drama, gossip, and politics.

24. Reflect on successes and misses and what you need to change and repeat.

25. Create intentional course corrections where you reset your flight path.

26. Stop worrying about what someone thinks. If you care about their opinion, ask them so you can react, or don't think about it.

27. Assume everyone thinks you are great and your work is great. React to evidence and reality, not what is in your head.

28. Take naps, and build in recovery sleep when you are exhausted.

29. Take failure as a stepping-stone to your ultimate success; you can't fail if you don't try.

30. Build a community where you want to belong; find people who energize and inspire you.

31. Be here, right now. Pay attention to where you are and leave distractions behind.

32. Stop trying to be something you are not; work on where you are now and where you want to be in a year.

33. Breathe.

34. Breathe again.

35. Breathe again. Three breaths always give you perspective and help you decide where you want to expend your energy.

36. Start a difficult conversation with "My intention is . . ." and be honest about your intentions.

37. If you are vulnerable and candid, it is contagious.

38. Build in recovery time from a demanding project when you hit a deadline. You can't run a marathon like a series of 200 meter sprints.

39. Say what you really want to say, not what you think the other person wants to hear.
40. If you pre-worry, learn to adequately prepare and then forget about it.
41. If you parallel-worry, notice it, let it go, and focus on really listening in the moment.
42. If you post-worry, spend a few minutes reflecting, identify patterns and evidence-backed insights, and then just forget about it.
43. Collect then share your thoughts and intent when having difficult conversations.
44. Act like you are about to quit but no one yet knows. What would you say and do if you were on your way out of the door?
45. Share why you are excited with your team.
46. Watch your tone—have you heard yourself lately? Are you energized and inspired yourself? Either way it is contagious.
47. Talk about five years into the future with your team. If they don't know the destination, how can they enjoy the journey?
48. Play opposites: If you're always the first to speak in a meeting, practice holding back and letting others speak; if you always point out the faults and downsides, practice looking on the bright side.
49. Know whether you understand and believe, and then help your team do the same.
50. Talk about your failures and your flaws, and then share what you learned.
51. Analyze your successes and learn how to replicate them.
52. Call your "Friday inspiration fix friends"; spend an hour every Friday calling people who energize and inspire you.
53. If you experience disappointment, shake it off fast and move forward.
54. Identify a new mentor when you move into a new job, company, or phase in your life.
55. Be specific with your mentor about how you want to gain their expertise—through storytelling, joint problem solving, question and answer, or something else.
56. Identify an inner circle of advisors who will be your truth-tellers.
57. Ask trusted peers to watch out and give you feedback if your energy is waning.
58. Know what boosts your energy and build that into your day.

59. Identify the doubters and extract yourself from time spent around them.

60. You are like a sponge; you absorb the energy of those around you, so surround yourself with positive, aspirational, and optimistic people.

61. Don't fall for repetitive resolution syndrome. If you didn't achieve your resolutions last year, stop to understand why before you repeat them.

62. Dedicate me-time to yourself each month.

63. Create your lost discipline list.

64. Decide if your wishes are empty or intentional and don't kid yourself.

65. Turn off the editor in your head, say exactly what you are thinking with no filter.

66. Make a commitment to your own daily and weekly rituals.

67. Decide what vacations you need each year; each December block them off for the next year.

68. Book time for every one of your family's birthdays and celebrate with them.

69. Whether you're a parent, auntie, uncle, or grandparent, spend one-on-one time with the children in your life, even for the smallest tasks or outings.

70. Find your favorite music and swap out your songs when your situation changes.

71. Don't expend energy on questions and topics that you cannot influence.

72. Find the very best people at the top of their game in your field of expertise and ask, "How can I replicate that so it works for me?"

73. Agree how you will fight before the battle starts.

74. Don't pretend to be someone you are not; it is too exhausting.

75. Rate your current role on a scale of 1 to 10: how energizing and inspiring is it, and how can you make it a 10?

76. What is your wishful thinking for how your life will be in three years?

77. Slam the brakes on if you slide down the downward spiral of gloom.

78. Eeyores love talking to other Eeyores; don't feed their misery.

79. Optimism and pessimism are contagious, so consciously decide what you want to spread.

80. Know what you want your legacy to be.

81. Don't create a Rolls Royce solution when a Mini will do.
82. Is your energy spent on reactive or proactive tasks?
83. Do you focus on individually driven goals or company-driven goals?
84. Company, team, individual—in what order do you and your team place your priority?
85. Know your typical reaction to change and adapt accordingly,
86. Intentionally sequence where you focus your energy.
87. Know who energizes and inspires you and who drains you; target your focus.
88. Tackle the knowledge, skills, and behavior your team needs to accelerate your growth.
89. Focus your efforts on the long-term results you want to achieve.
90. Spend spontaneous time with your team, getting curious about their work, their projects, and their lives.
91. When you make an error, state it, share it, and learn from it.
92. When you are exhausted focus solely on the essential and time sensitive; schedule in time to recharge.
93. Ask for help when you need it and return the favor when others ask.
94. Book your travel to optimize your comfort and sleep, not to save $50.
95. Cheap hotels and coach flights are mentally draining; give your energy a boost by upgrading and not taking the cheapest option.
96. Prior to crunch time, charge up your reserves so you have backup energy to carry you through.
97. During crunch time invest in extra help so your energy can be spent on the crucial activities that only you can do.
98. Use a journal to capture your thoughts and feelings.
99. Smile. It is contagious.

NINETY-NINE WAYS TO BE THOUGHTFULLY RUTHLESS WITH YOUR RESOURCES

1. Make a fast decision on your team members if you are unsure they will make it.
2. Identify 25 percent of your current activities that you can delegate to others on your team.
3. Identify your noncore activities that you can outsource.
4. Never assemble your own furniture again.

5. Hire a cleaner.
6. Use the laundry services of your local dry-cleaner.
7. Use a concierge service or virtual administrator to help with household administration tasks you don't need to do yourself.
8. Ask for referrals to save time researching new service providers.
9. Use task rabbit to hire helping hands.
10. Conduct a meeting review every Monday morning, and cancel, delegate, or decline 20 percent of your meetings.
11. Align your rewards to accelerate company, not individual, goals.
12. Conduct a quarterly resources rebalance to align your best people to your top priorities.
13. If you don't have two successors identified, create a plan to identify them.
14. For creation, writing, and uninterrupted work, get an "air-gap PC," not connected to the Internet and without your favorite apps.
15. Know if you are about to enter an intentional-annoyance phase with your team and don't overreact to it.
16. In times of uncertainty, don't ask for feedback until you have something your teams can react to.
17. Treat your board of directors like an extension of your team; know when you need to raise the expectations for what they are delivering.
18. Tell trusted colleagues what your personal development goals are, and ask them to hold you accountable.
19. Help your team know what messages to amplify out to their teams and what to absorb.
20. Overhire your team. Hire the expertise you need to run your business according to the size and scale it will be in five years.
21. Galvanize your team around a common goal.
22. Know your percent-sure-and-go number: tell your team how sure they need to be before they act. 70 percent? 51 percent?
23. Surprise and delight your team in how you communicate.
24. Use video, pictures, or real or virtual news clippings to share your message.
25. Focus on the one thing—what is your one message, your one action, your one priority? Share this with your team.
26. Forget PowerPoint; if you are spending more time figuring out animations and shapes, you have lost the point of your conversation.

27. Focus on developing the skills of your people managers to actually manage people.
28. Set clear expectations for how you want people managers to lead.
29. Set up forums in which your people managers can learn, share, and practice how to lead others.
30. Put people in roles that play to their strengths.
31. Set reviews for your new hires after 90 days.
32. Create launch plans for your new employees that focus on first month, first quarter, and first year in the job.
33. Exit mismatched employees swiftly and with grace.
34. Focus your recognition and rewards on what you want to replicate.
35. Set up breakfast with your new hires each month to listen and learn.
36. Regularly meet with your contrarian employees; ask them what is holding you back from achieving your strategy and goals.
37. Set up a cash incentive employee referral program and proactively ask and follow up with referrals.
38. Use interns to bring in an infusion of fresh ideas.
39. Don't invest in team building and strategy sessions until your leadership team is the right team in place.
40. Before giving feedback, ask whether it is a good time.
41. Remember to say thank you to your team, and mean it.
42. Reflect on the last seven days—apply some gratitude.
43. Write handwritten notes of thanks once a month.
44. Recognize employees' length of service at company meetings.
45. Make sure your virtual you represents the real you—Google yourself and see.
46. Audio record your all-employee meetings, or your thoughts after a customer visit or international site trip.
47. Use a translation service like rev.com to automatically transcribe audio recordings of your speeches and presentations and share them with your organization.
48. Use the dictation feature on your laptop to listen to your writing and e-mails before you send them.
49. Learn power writing: use examples, metaphors, and stories.
50. Be a role model thoughtfully ruthless leader.
51. Push ownership for decisions down to the lowest possible level.
52. Create tenets for how decisions are made.

53. Conduct spontaneous telephone interviews so you get the real person, not the overly prepared and poised person.
54. Measure and share progress of key results regularly with your team.
55. Triple the investment in your recruitment team for the short term to get your new hires in faster and boost your productivity.
56. Only have one "development-in-progress" person on your team at once, if that.
57. Act in the way you want your team to replicate.
58. Teach the art of leadership to new managers.
59. Set high expectations and standards.
60. Stand your ground when you need to support your team.
61. Ask your team to tell you each month who you need to get to know on their team.
62. Don't force fun.
63. Avoid team-building activities that involve physical activities, danger, and labeling people based on their personality.
64. Know who you are developing as your successor and aggressively invest in them.
65. Always have a "waiting list" of key talent ready for when you have an opening on your team.
66. Ask who is a blocker to others' progressing and getting promoted; move them out of the way.
67. Listen for gossip, speculation, and hearsay—and eradicate it.
68. Hire where your talent is, not where your headquarters is. Be flexible.
69. Don't send e-mails that require scrolling down the page.
70. Know the cost of meetings and make sure there is a return on investment with decisions and impact.
71. Accelerate a new leader's performance by interviewing him in front of his team so they know everything they need to know about him to accelerate trust.
72. If you want cross-group collaboration, do not reward individual performance.
73. Follow the ABC of disagreements: Air your points of view, bear other people's perspectives in mind, and commit to the decision.
74. Focus on your strengths and sharing them with others rather than trying to fix what you are not great at.
75. Build a team that fills the gaps in areas you don't enjoy.

76. Never move a problem employee to get them off your team.
77. Help your boss or board know who the superstars are in your organization.
78. Know how strong your pipeline is for the leaders and experts you will need on your future team.
79. Don't issue ego invites to meetings.
80. Match your top people to your most important projects.
81. Create the space to allow innovation.
82. Sunset projects fast if they don't meet your goals.
83. Create an infusion of the voice of youth in your products through testing, focus groups, and teenage immersion.
84. Spend more time evaluating long-term bets and strategic choices than executing on existing projects.
85. Surround yourself with candid truth-tellers, not yes men and women.
86. Understand and share the decision dilemmas you have in your organization.
87. Help your team keep their blinders to leap over fences and win the race without getting distracted.
88. Create a memorable beginning and a dramatic end to any talk or presentation you give.
89. To become more memorable, tell stories to get your message across.
90. Create an annual calendar of influence for how you manage your relationships and results with customers, partners, and investors throughout the year.
91. Consciously manage your cultural continuum, intentionally leaving behind and embracing new factors as you grow.
92. Don't sheep dip new acquisitions into the cultural way you do everything—learn and absorb their best parts and tailor your marriage intentionally.
93. Reward innovation attempts.
94. Promote failed projects and share lessons in a nonjudgmental way.
95. Teach everyone ROE, return on effort. Investments and energy need business impact.
96. Manage the symbiotic relationship between your technical, creative, and business talent to catapult growth and innovation.
97. Teaching is the fastest way to learn something new; create teaching opportunities for your team.

98. Take a seat and observe where your teams sit. Is it inspiring, comfortable, and conducive to experimentation?
99. Reward your experts for being experts; don't force them to manage people to get a pay rise.

ABOUT THE AUTHOR

Val Wright, internationally acclaimed innovation expert, was named as one of the top 50 resources for Chief Operating Officers by ClickSoftware. She is one of only 64 experts inducted into Million Dollar Consultant® Hall of Fame. The global clients who have requested her help include Starbucks, LinkedIn, Microsoft, Financial Times, and DreamWorks Animation. Val's corporate experience includes tenures during dramatic growth periods at Amazon, BMW, Microsoft, Harrods, Marconi, and Sema Group.

Val participated on the small team that created the fastest selling device of all time, Kinect for Xbox, which won a Guinness book of world records selling over 20 million devices. This contributed to the turnaround of Microsoft's Entertainment business from a billion-dollar loss to a multi-million-dollar profit machine.

Her unique approach, which she has trademarked as Thoughtfully Ruthless™, has produced typical clients, results of market domination in extraordinarily short timeframes along with compassionate truth telling, fearlessness, and extensive creative, technical, and leadership gains.

She is a regular contributor on CNBC, *Inc.*, *Business Insider*, *Fast Company*, *Bloomberg*, *Reuters*, *LA Times*, MSN, and *Today*.

Originally from England, Val now lives in California with her twin five-year-olds, seven-year-old daughter, and husband.

INDEX